# The SAS® Workbook Solutions

Ron Cody

The correct bibliographic citation for this manual is as follows: Cody, Ron. 1996. *The SAS® Workbook Solutions*. Cary, NC: SAS Institute Inc.

**The SAS® Workbook Solutions**



ISBN 978-1-55544-758-8



SAS Institute Inc., SAS Campus Drive, Cary, North Carolina 27513.

1st printing, February 1996
2nd printing, June 1996
3rd printing, December 1996
4th printing, May 1997
5th printing, September 2006
6th printing, October 2007

# Table of Contents

# Preface

*The SAS Workbook Solutions* is the companion to *The SAS Workbook.* As you look through the solutions, realize that most of the problems can be solved in a variety of ways. Some of the problems have more than one solution provided. Your solution may differ from mine, and that is OK. Be sure to print out resulting data sets to be sure your solutions are correct. You may want to compare your data sets to those produced by the solutions presented here. Some of the solutions in this book contain labels, formats, or both, that are not specifically requested in the problem. They are included to make the output more readable, but don't think that your solution is wrong just because of these extra "bells and whistles" in some of my solutions.

You may also be interested in the relative efficiency of different solutions. Try running alternative solutions and check the processing times. You may need to turn off your disk caching program to make a fair comparison of times.

The solutions in this book assume that all external raw data files, as well as permanent SAS data sets and format libraries, are located in a subdirectory called C:\WORKBOOK. If you are running SAS in a different operating environment or have placed your data sets elsewhere, simply make the appropriate changes to the solutions.

One final note. Be sure to make a concerted effort to solve the problems before looking in this book for the solution. You will learn much more that way.

RPC

Spring 1996

# CHAPTER 1 Inputting Raw Data

## SOLUTION TO PROBLEM 1

```
DATA CLASS;
   INPUT F_NAME $ ID $ GENDER $ GPA HEIGHT WEIGHT;
DATALINES;
Hector      123      M         3.5     59         155
Nancy       328      F         3.7     52          99
Edward      747      M         2.4     62         205
Michelle    778      F         3.0     54         115
Sampson     289      M         3.5     60         180
;
PROC PRINT DATA=CLASS;
   TITLE 'Listing of CLASS data set';
RUN;
```

## SOLUTION TO PROBLEM 2

```
DATA CLASS;
   INPUT F_NAME $ ID $ GENDER $ GPA HEIGHT WEIGHT;
DATALINES;
George      123      M         3.5     .          155
.           328      F         3.7     52          99
Edward      747      .         .       .           .
Michelle    778      F         3.0     54          .
Sampson     289      M         3.5     60         180
;
PROC PRINT DATA=CLASS;
   TITLE 'Listing of CLASS data set';
RUN;
```

## SOLUTION TO PROBLEM 3

```
DATA CLASS;
   INFORMAT F_NAME $10.;

  /*-------------------------------------------------------*
   | Two alternative solutions are:                         |
   |                                                        |
   | LENGTH F_NAME $ 10;                                    |
   |         or                                             |
   | INPUT F_NAME : $10. ID $ GENDER $ GPA HEIGHT WEIGHT;   |
   *-------------------------------------------------------*/

   INPUT F_NAME $ ID $ GENDER $ GPA HEIGHT WEIGHT;
DATALINES;
Hector      123      M         3.5     59         155
Nancy       328      F         3.7     52          99
Edward      747      M         2.4     62         205
Michelle    778      F         3.0     54         115
Washington  289      M         3.5     60         180
;
PROC PRINT DATA=CLASS;
   TITLE 'Listing of CLASS data set';
RUN;
```

## SOLUTION TO PROBLEM 4

```
DATA CLASS;
*-------------------------------------------------------------*
| The key here is to use the MISSOVER option which says that  |
| if you reach the end of a data line and have not yet read   |
| values for all your variables, set all the remaining values |
| to missing.                                                 |
*-------------------------------------------------------------*;
```

```
   INFILE DATALINES MISSOVER;
*-------------------------------------------------------------*
| Try running this program without the MISSOVER option to see |
| what happens.                                               |
*-------------------------------------------------------------*;

   INPUT F_NAME $ ID $ GENDER $ GPA HEIGHT WEIGHT;
DATALINES;
George      123     M       3.5     .       155
.           328     F       3.7     52       99
Edward      747
Michelle    778     F       3.0     54
Sampson     289     M       3.5     60      180
;
PROC PRINT DATA=CLASS;
   TITLE 'Listing of CLASS data set';
RUN;
```

**SOLUTION TO PROBLEM 5**

```
DATA CLASS;
*-------------------------------------------------------------*
| The key here is to use the DSD option which allows you to   |
| read comma-delimited data, to treat 2 consecutive commas as |
| a missing value, and to remove the double quotes from quoted|
| strings.                                                    |
*-------------------------------------------------------------*;
   INFILE DATALINES DSD;

   INPUT F_NAME $ ID $ GENDER $ GPA HEIGHT WEIGHT;
DATALINES;
George,123,M,3.5,,155
,328,"F",3.7,52,99
"Edward",747,,,,
Michelle,778,F,3.0,54,,
Sampson,289,M,3.5,60,180
;
PROC PRINT DATA=CLASS;
   TITLE 'Listing of CLASS data set';
RUN;
```

**SOLUTION TO PROBLEM 6**

```
DATA CLASS;
   INPUT     F_NAME $   1-8
             ID     $   13-15
             GENDER $   22
             GPA        31-33
             HEIGHT     39-40
             WEIGHT     49-51;
DATALINES;
George      123     M       3.5     59      155
Nancy       328     F       3.7     52       99
Edward      747     M       2.4     62      205
Michelle    778     F       3.0     54      115
Sampson     289     M       3.5     60      180
;
PROC PRINT DATA=CLASS;
   TITLE 'Listing of CLASS data set';
RUN;
```

**SOLUTION TO PROBLEM 7**

```
DATA CLASS;
*-------------------------------------------------------------*
| Use the PAD option to be sure that the SAS System will not  |
| try to read data from the next line.  The need for this     |
| option will vary depending on which version of SAS Software |
| you are running.  It is a good idea to use the PAD option   |
| when reading fixed records from an external file.           |
*-------------------------------------------------------------*;
   INFILE DATALINES PAD;

   INPUT F_NAME $ 1-8 ID $ 13-15 GENDER $ 22 GPA 31-33 HEIGHT 39-40
         WEIGHT 49-51;
DATALINES;
George      123      M        3.5                155
            328      F        3.7      52         99
Edward      747
Michelle    778      F        3.0      54
Sampson     289      M        3.5      60        180
;
PROC PRINT DATA=CLASS;
   TITLE 'Listing of CLASS data set';
RUN;
```

**SOLUTION TO PROBLEM 8**

```
DATA CLASS;
   INPUT @1    F_NAME     $8.
         @13   ID         $3.
         @22   GENDER     $1.
         @31   GPA         3.
         @39   HEIGHT      2.
         @49   WEIGHT      3.;
DATALINES;
George      123      M        3.5      59        155
Nancy       328      F        3.7      52         99
Edward      747      M        2.4      62        205
Michelle    778      F        3.0      54        115
Sampson     289      M        3.5      60        180
;
PROC PRINT DATA=CLASS;
   TITLE 'Listing of CLASS data set';
RUN;
```

**SOLUTION TO PROBLEM 9**

```
DATA SURVEY;
   INPUT YEAR $ 15-18  @; *** Hold the line;
   IF YEAR = '1994' THEN
      INPUT ID      $ 1-3
            GENDER $ 4
            PARTY  $ 5
            VOTE   $ 6
            NUM_TV   7-8;
   ELSE IF YEAR = '1995' THEN
      INPUT ID      $ 1-3
            AGE       4-5
            GENDER $ 6
            PARTY  $ 7
            VOTE   $ 8
            NUM_TV   9-10;
```

```
DATALINES;
001MRY 3      1994
00923FDY 1    1995
012FDN 2      1994
00518MRN 2    1995
003MDY 4      1994
;
PROC PRINT;
   TITLE 'Listing of SURVEY Data set';
RUN;
```

**SOLUTION TO PROBLEM 10**

```
DATA SURVEY;
   INPUT #1     SUBJECT  $ 1-3
             @4 DOB        MMDDYY8.
                STATE    $ 25-26
                ZIP_CODE $ 40-44
          #2    NUMBER          5
                CAR1     $ 11-20
                CAR2     $ 21-30;
  /*-----------------------------------------------------*
   |   Alternative Code:                                 |
   |                                                     |
   |   INPUT #1 @1   SUBJECT      $3.                    |
   |            @4   DOB     MMDDYY8.                    |
   |            @25  STATE        $2.                    |
   |            @40  ZIP_CODE     $5.                    |
   |         #2 @5   NUMBER        5.                    |
   |            @11  CAR1        $10.                    |
   |            @21  CAR2        $10.;                   |
   *-----------------------------------------------------*/

   FORMAT DOB MMDDYY8.;
DATALINES;
12310/21/46             NJ              08822
123 2     Ford      Oldsmobile
23711/01/55             NY              11518
237 1     Chevy
;
PROC PRINT DATA=SURVEY;
   TITLE 'Listing of SURVEY data set';
RUN;
```

**SOLUTION TO PROBLEM 11**

```
DATA TEMPER;
   INPUT TEMP @@;
DATALINES;
21  23   29 33 19  28
33  39 43  44 28  21 24    27  29
37   32    31  33 29
;
PROC PRINT;
   TITLE 'Listing of TEMPER data set';
RUN;
```

**SOLUTION TO PROBLEM 12**

```
DATA TEMP_DAY;
   INPUT DAY TEMP @@;
DATALINES;
5 21  6  23   7  29 8 33 9 19  10  28
11  33  12  39 13  43  14   44 15 28  16 21 17 24   18 27 19   29
20 37  21 32  22  31 23 33  24 29
;
```

```
PROC PRINT;
   TITLE 'Listing of TEMP_DAY data set';
RUN;
```

### SOLUTION TO PROBLEM 13

```
DATA RATS;
   INPUT GROUP $ WEIGHT @@;
DATALINES;
A 34  B 58   A 28  C 55
C 56  A 27   B 52  C 58  A 21  B 62
;
PROC PRINT;
   TITLE 'Listing of RATS data set';
RUN;
```

### SOLUTION TO PROBLEM 14

```
DATA RATS;
   LENGTH GROUP $ 1;
   RETAIN GROUP;
   INPUT DUMMY $ @@;
   IF DUMMY IN ('A','B','C') THEN DO;
      GROUP = DUMMY;
      DELETE;
      RETURN; *** RETURN not needed but OK to have;
   END;
   *** Wind up here only if a weight is read;
   WEIGHT = INPUT (DUMMY,8.); *** Convert WEIGHT to numeric;
   OUTPUT;
   DROP DUMMY;
DATALINES;
A 34  28   B 58  52
62  C 55   A 27 21
C  56  58
;
PROC PRINT;
   TITLE 'Listing of RATS data set';
RUN;
```

### SOLUTION TO PROBLEM 15

```
DATA VARLIST;
   INPUT @1  (Q1-Q5)(2.)
         @15 (DATE1-DATE3)(MMDDYY8.)
         @50 (X1-X3 Y1-Y3)($1.);
   FORMAT DATE1-DATE3 MMDDYY8.;
DATALINES;
1122334455    10/21/4611/13/4206/05/48          123456
9672347656    01/01/9501/02/9501/03/95          987654
;
PROC PRINT;
   TITLE 'Listing of VARLIST data set';
RUN;
```

### SOLUTION TO PROBLEM 16

```
DATA POINTER;
   INPUT @1  (X1-X3)(2. +5)
         @3  (Y1-Y3)(2. +5)
         @5  (Z1-Z3)($3. +4);
DATALINES;
0102AAA0304BBB0506CCC
2837ABC9676DEF8765GHI
;
```

```
PROC PRINT;
   TITLE 'Listing of POINTER data set';
RUN;
```

# CHAPTER 2 Reading and Writing from External Files

## SOLUTION TO PROBLEM 1

```
DATA CARS;
   INFILE 'C:\WORKBOOK\CARS.DTA' PAD;
*-------------------------------------------------------------*
| The PAD option may not be necessary but it is a good idea   |
| to include it, especially if there are short records in the |
| external file.                                              |
*-------------------------------------------------------------*;

  /*-----------------------------------------*
   | Alternate method:                        |
   |                                          |
   | FILENAME CAR 'C:\WORKBOOK\CARS.DTA';     |
   | INFILE CAR PAD;                          |
   *-----------------------------------------*/

   INPUT  @ 1 SIZE     $9.
          @11 MANUFACT $9.
          @22 MODEL    $9.
          @38 MILEAGE   2.
          @50 RELIABLE  1.;
RUN;

PROC PRINT DATA=CARS;
   TITLE 'Listing of CARS Data Set';
RUN;
```

## SOLUTION TO PROBLEM 2

```
DATA DEMOG_12;
   IF FILE1 = 0 THEN INFILE 'C:\WORKBOOK\DEMOG1.DTA' END=FILE1;
   ELSE INFILE 'C:\WORKBOOK\DEMOG2.DTA';
   INPUT  @1  ID       $3.
          @4  DOB       MMDDYY6.
          @10 GENDER   $1.
          @11 STATE    $2.
          @13 EMPLOYED $1.;
   FORMAT DOB MMDDYY8.;
RUN;


PROC PRINT DATA=DEMOG_12;
   TITLE 'Listing of DEMOG_12 Data Set';
RUN;
```

## SOLUTION TO PROBLEM 3

```
DATA DEMOG_12;
   INPUT RAWFILE $ 1-25;
   INFILE DUMMY FILEVAR=RAWFILE END=LASTREC;
   DO UNTIL (LASTREC=1);
      INPUT  @1  ID       $3.
             @4  DOB       MMDDYY6.
             @10 GENDER   $1.
             @11 STATE    $2.
             @13 EMPLOYED $1.;
      OUTPUT;
   FORMAT DOB MMDDYY8.;
   END;
DATALINES;
C:\WORKBOOK\DEMOG1.DTA
C:\WORKBOOK\DEMOG2.DTA
RUN;
```

```
PROC PRINT DATA=DEMOG_12;
   TITLE 'Listing of DEMOG_12 Data Set';
RUN;
```

# CHAPTER 3 Using Logical Structures: IF-THEN/ELSE, WHERE, and SELECT

## SOLUTION TO PROBLEM 1

```
DATA RECODE;
   INFILE 'C:\WORKBOOK\DEMOG1.DTA' PAD;
   INPUT  @1  ID       $3.
          @4  DOB       MMDDYY6.
          @10 GENDER   $1.
          @11 STATE    $2.
          @13 EMPLOYED $1.;

*-----------------------------------------------------------------*
| Note: AGE computed in the next line is approximate and may     |
| be incorrect if a visit is on a patient's birthday, depending  |
| on whether the current year is a leap year and how many leap   |
| years have occurred between the date of birth and the current  |
| date.                                                           |
*-----------------------------------------------------------------*;
   AGE = ROUND (('01JAN96'D - DOB)/365.25);
   IF 0 LE AGE LE 20 THEN       AGEGROUP = 1;
   ELSE IF 21 LE AGE LE 40 THEN AGEGROUP = 2;
   ELSE IF 41 LE AGE LE 60 THEN AGEGROUP = 3;
   ELSE IF AGE GT 60 THEN       AGEGROUP = 4;
FORMAT DOB MMDDYY8.;
RUN;


PROC PRINT DATA=RECODE;
   TITLE 'Listing of Data Set RECODE';
RUN;
```

## SOLUTION TO PROBLEM 2

```
*----------------------------------------------------------------*
| Brute force method (i.e. straightforward)                      |
*----------------------------------------------------------------*;
DATA CAR_INX;
   INFILE 'C:\WORKBOOK\CARS.DTA' PAD;
   INPUT  @1  SIZE     $9.
          @11 MANUFACT $9.
          @22 MODEL    $9.
          @38 MILEAGE   2.
          @50 RELIABLE  1.;

   IF SIZE = 'SMALL' THEN DO;
      IF 0 LE MILEAGE LE 20 THEN DO;
         IF 1 LE RELIABLE LE 3 THEN INDEX = 1;
         ELSE IF 4 LE RELIABLE LE 5 THEN INDEX = 2;
      END;
      ELSE IF 21 LE MILEAGE LE 50 THEN DO;
         IF 1 LE RELIABLE LE 3 THEN INDEX = 3;
         ELSE IF 4 LE RELIABLE LE 5 THEN INDEX = 4;
      END;
   END;

   ELSE IF SIZE = 'COMPACT' THEN DO;
      IF 0 LE MILEAGE LE 15 THEN DO;
         IF 1 LE RELIABLE LE 3 THEN INDEX = 1;
         ELSE IF 4 LE RELIABLE LE 5 THEN INDEX = 2;
      END;
```

```
         ELSE IF 16 LE MILEAGE LE 50 THEN DO;
            IF 1 LE RELIABLE LE 3 THEN INDEX = 3;
            ELSE IF 4 LE RELIABLE LE 5 THEN INDEX = 4;
         END;
      END;

      ELSE IF SIZE = 'MID-SIZED' THEN DO;
         IF 0 LE MILEAGE LE 12 THEN DO;
            IF 1 LE RELIABLE LE 3 THEN INDEX = 1;
            ELSE IF 4 LE RELIABLE LE 5 THEN INDEX = 2;
         END;
         ELSE IF 13 LE MILEAGE LE 50 THEN DO;
            IF 1 LE RELIABLE LE 3 THEN INDEX = 3;
            ELSE IF 4 LE RELIABLE LE 5 THEN INDEX = 4;
         END;
      END;
RUN;

PROC PRINT DATA=CAR_INX;
   TITLE 'Listing of Data Set CAR_INX';
RUN;


 /*-----------------------------------------------------------------*
   | Alternative Solution: A bit fancier (and shorter)              |
   |                                                                |
   | DATA CAR_INX;                                                  |
   |    INFILE 'C:\WORKBOOK\CARS.DTA' PAD;                          |
   |    INPUT  @1  SIZE     $9.                                     |
   |           @11 MANUFACT $9.                                     |
   |           @22 MODEL    $9.                                     |
   |           @38 MILEAGE   2.                                     |
   |           @50 RELIABLE  1.;                                    |
   |                                                                |
   |    ***Initialize INDEX to either 0 or 1 based on reliability;  |
   |    IF 1 LE RELIABLE LE 3 THEN INDEX = 0;                       |
   |    ELSE IF 4 LE RELIABLE LE 5 THEN INDEX = 1;                  |
   |                                                                |
   |    ***Set the upper limit of mileage for lower INDEX values;   |
   |    IF SIZE = 'SMALL' THEN UPPER = 20;                          |
   |    ELSE IF SIZE = 'COMPACT' THEN UPPER = 15;                   |
   |    ELSE IF SIZE = 'MID-SIZED' THEN UPPER = 12;                 |
   |                                                                |
   |    ***Finally, compute the INDEX;                              |
   |    IF 0 LE MILEAGE LE UPPER THEN INDEX = INDEX + 1;            |
   |    ELSE IF MILEAGE NE . THEN     INDEX = INDEX + 3;            |
   |                                                                |
   |    DROP UPPER;                                                 |
   | RUN;                                                           |
   |                                                                |
   | PROC PRINT DATA=CAR_INX;                                       |
   |    TITLE 'Test Print of Data Set CAR_INX';                     |
   | RUN;                                                           |
   |                                                                |
   *----------------------------------------------------------------*/
```

## SOLUTION TO PROBLEM 3

```
*---------------------------------------------------------------*
| Note: There are LOTS of other correct solutions.              |
*---------------------------------------------------------------*;
DATA CAR_INX;
   INFILE 'C:\WORKBOOK\CARS.DTA' PAD;
```

```
   INPUT @1  SIZE     $9.
         @11 MANUFACT $9.
         @22 MODEL    $9.
         @38 MILEAGE   2.
         @50 RELIABLE  1.;

   SELECT;
      WHEN (1 LE RELIABLE LE 3) INDEX = 0;
      WHEN (4 LE RELIABLE LE 5) INDEX = 1;
      OTHERWISE;
   END;

   SELECT;
      WHEN (SIZE = 'SMALL')     UPPER = 20;
      WHEN (SIZE = 'COMPACT')   UPPER = 15;
      WHEN (SIZE = 'MID_SIZED') UPPER = 12;
      OTHERWISE;

   END;

   SELECT;
      WHEN (0 LE MILEAGE LE UPPER)      INDEX = INDEX + 1;
      WHEN (MILEAGE NE .)               INDEX = INDEX + 3;
      OTHERWISE;
   END;
   DROP UPPER;
RUN;

PROC PRINT DATA=CAR_INX;
   TITLE 'Listing of Data Set CAR_INX';
RUN;
```

## SOLUTION TO PROBLEM 4

```
*--------------------------------------------------------------*
|The FMTSEARCH= system option is needed because there are      |
|permanently assigned formats in this data set.  You could,    |
|alternatively, use the default format library name LIBRARY and|
|omit this statement                                           |
*--------------------------------------------------------------*;
LIBNAME WORKBOOK 'C:\WORKBOOK';
OPTIONS FMTSEARCH=(WORKBOOK);

DATA HYPERTEN;
   SET WORKBOOK.CLINICAL(KEEP=GENDER DBP SBP VISIT DOB);
   AGE = INT((VISIT - DOB)/365.25);

   IF 0 LE AGE LE 30 THEN DO;
      IF GENDER = 'M' THEN DO;
         D_LIMIT = 88;
         S_LIMIT = 152;
      END;
      ELSE IF GENDER = 'F' THEN DO;
         D_LIMIT = 86;
         S_LIMIT = 150;
      END;
   END;

   ELSE IF 31 LE AGE LE 65 THEN DO;
      IF GENDER = 'M' THEN DO;
         D_LIMIT = 92;
         S_LIMIT = 162;
      END;
```

```
      ELSE IF GENDER = 'F' THEN DO;
         D_LIMIT = 88;
         S_LIMIT = 158;
      END;
   END;

   ELSE IF AGE GE 66 THEN DO;
      IF GENDER = 'M' THEN DO;
         D_LIMIT = 94;
         S_LIMIT = 166;
      END;
      ELSE IF GENDER = 'F' THEN DO;
         D_LIMIT = 92;
         S_LIMIT = 164;
      END;
   END;

   IF DBP GT D_LIMIT OR SBP GT S_LIMIT THEN HYPER = 'Y';
      ELSE IF DBP NE . AND SBP NE . THEN    HYPER = 'N';

   DROP D_LIMIT S_LIMIT VISIT DOB;
RUN;


PROC PRINT DATA=HYPERTEN;
   TITLE 'Test Print of Data Set HYPER';
RUN;


 /*-----------------------------------------------------------*
  | Alternative solution:                                      |
  |                                                            |
  | DATA HYPERTEN;                                             |
  |    SET WORKBOOK.CLINICAL(KEEP=GENDER DBP SBP VISIT DOB);   |
  |                                                            |
  |    AGE = INT((VISIT - DOB)/365.25);                        |
  |                                                            |
  |    IF 0 LE AGE LE 30 AND GENDER = 'M' THEN DO;             |
  |       D_LIMIT = 88;                                        |
  |       S_LIMIT = 152;                                       |
  |    END;                                                    |
  |                                                            |
  |    ELSE IF 0 LE AGE LE 30 AND GENDER = 'F' THEN DO;        |
  |       D_LIMIT = 86;                                        |
  |       S_LIMIT = 150;                                       |
  |    END;                                                    |
  |                                                            |
  |    ELSE IF 31 LE AGE LE 65 AND GENDER = 'M' THEN DO;       |
  |       D_LIMIT = 92;                                        |
  |       S_LIMIT = 162;                                       |
  |    END;                                                    |
  |                                                            |
  |    ELSE IF 31 LE AGE LE 65 AND GENDER = 'F' THEN DO;       |
  |       D_LIMIT = 88;                                        |
  |       S_LIMIT = 158;                                       |
  |    END;                                                    |
  |                                                            |
  |    ELSE IF AGE GE 66 AND GENDER = 'M' THEN DO;             |
  |       D_LIMIT = 94;                                        |
  |       S_LIMIT = 166;                                       |
  |    END;                                                    |
  |                                                            |
```

```
|    ELSE IF AGE GE 66 AND GENDER = 'F' THEN DO;               |
|       D_LIMIT = 92;                                          |
|       S_LIMIT = 164;                                         |
|    END;                                                      |
|                                                              |
|    IF DBP GT D_LIMIT OR SBP GT S_LIMIT THEN HYPER = 'Y';     |
|       ELSE IF DBP NE . AND SBP NE . THEN    HYPER = 'N';     |
|                                                              |
|    DROP D_LIMIT S_LIMIT VISIT DOB;                           |
| RUN;                                                         |
|                                                              |
| PROC PRINT DATA=HYPERTEN;                                    |
|    TITLE 'Test Print of Data Set HYPER';                     |
| RUN;                                                         |
*--------------------------------------------------------------*/
```

# CHAPTER 4 Combining SAS® Data Sets

## SOLUTION TO PROBLEM 1

```
DATA PAY1995;
   LENGTH ID $ 3 GENDER $ 1;
   INPUT ID LEVEL SALARY GENDER;
   FORMAT SALARY DOLLAR8.;
DATALINES;
A23 32 68000 M
A24 35 75000 F
A30 44 97000 M
A13 28 27000 F
;
DATA PAY1996;
   LENGTH ID $ 3 GENDER $ 1;
   INPUT ID LEVEL SALARY GENDER;
   FORMAT SALARY DOLLAR8.;
DATALINES;
A25 29 35000 F
A26 36 88000 F
;
DATA PAY95_96;
   SET PAY1995 PAY1996;
RUN;

PROC PRINT DATA=PAY95_96;
   TITLE 'Listing of Data Set PAY95_96';
RUN;
```

## SOLUTION TO PROBLEM 2

```
*-----------------------------------------------------------*
| Create PAY1995 with code in PROBLEM 1                      |
*-----------------------------------------------------------*;
DATA FEM_1995;
   SET PAY1995;
   WHERE GENDER = 'F';
***Alternative: IF GENDER = 'F';
RUN;


PROC PRINT DATA=FEM_1995;
   TITLE 'Listing of Data Set FEM_1995';
RUN;
```

## SOLUTION TO PROBLEM 3

```
*-----------------------------------------------------------*
| Create PAY1995 with code in PROBLEM 1                      |
*-----------------------------------------------------------*;
DATA FEM_1995 MAL_1995;
   SET PAY1995;
   IF GENDER = 'F' THEN OUTPUT FEM_1995;
   ELSE IF GENDER = 'M' THEN OUTPUT MAL_1995;
RUN;

PROC PRINT DATA=FEM_1995;
   TITLE 'Listing of Data Set FEM_1995';
RUN;

PROC PRINT DATA=MAL_1995;
   TITLE 'Listing of Data Set MAL_1995';
RUN;
```

**SOLUTION TO PROBLEM 4**

```
LIBNAME WORKBOOK 'C:\WORKBOOK';
OPTIONS FMTSEARCH=(WORKBOOK);

*------------------------------------------------------------*
| Solution using the WHERE Statement                         |
*------------------------------------------------------------*;
DATA OLD_HYP;
   SET WORKBOOK.CLINICAL;
   WHERE DOB LT '01JAN70'D AND
         DOB NE .          AND
         (SBP GT 140       OR
         DBP GT 90);
RUN;

PROC PRINT DATA=OLD_HYP;
   TITLE 'Listing of Data Set OLD_HYP';
RUN;

 /*-------------------------------------------------------*
  | Alternative solution: Using a WHERE= Data Set Option   |
  |                                                        |
  | DATA OLD_HYP;                                          |
  |    SET WORKBOOK.CLINICAL (WHERE=(DOB LT '01JAN70'D AND |
  |                                  DOB NE . AND          |
  |                                  (SBP GT 140 OR        |
  |                                  DBP GT 90)));         |
  | RUN;                                                   |
  |                                                        |
  | PROC PRINT DATA=OLD_HYP;                               |
  |    TITLE 'Listing of Data Set OLD_HYP';                |
  | RUN;                                                   |
  *-------------------------------------------------------*/
```

**SOLUTION TO PROBLEM 5**

```
DATA CARS;
   INFILE 'C:\WORKBOOK\CARS.DTA' PAD;
   INPUT @ 1 SIZE     $9.
         @11 MANUFACT $9.
         @22 MODEL    $9.
         @38 MILEAGE   2.
         @50 RELIABLE  1.;
RUN;

DATA BEGIN_C;
   SET CARS;
   WHERE MODEL LIKE 'C%';
RUN;

PROC PRINT DATA=BEGIN_C;
   TITLE 'Listing of Data Set BEGIN_C';
RUN;

DATA BEGIN_C5;
   SET CARS;
   WHERE MODEL LIKE 'C____'; ***C followed by 4 underscores;
RUN;
```

```
PROC PRINT DATA=BEGIN_C5;
   TITLE 'Listing of Data Set BEGIN_C5';
RUN;
```

### SOLUTION TO PROBLEM 6

```
*-------------------------------------------------------------*
| Create PAY1995 with code in PROBLEM 1                       |
*-------------------------------------------------------------*;
DATA MER1995;
   LENGTH ID $ 3 MERIT $ 1;
   INPUT ID MERIT;
DATALINES;
A28 Y
A23 Y
A24 N
;
PROC SORT DATA=PAY1995;
   BY ID;
RUN;

PROC SORT DATA=MER1995;
   BY ID;
RUN;

DATA PAYM1995;
   MERGE PAY1995 MER1995;
   BY ID;
RUN;

PROC PRINT DATA=PAYM1995;
   TITLE 'Listing of Data Set PAYM1995';
RUN;
```

### SOLUTION TO PROBLEM 7

```
*-------------------------------------------------------------*
| Create PAY1995 with code in PROBLEM 1                       |
*-------------------------------------------------------------*;

*-------------------------------------------------------------*
| Compute the mean salary for males and females               |
*-------------------------------------------------------------*;
PROC MEANS DATA=PAY1995 NWAY NOPRINT;
   CLASS GENDER;
   VAR SALARY;
   OUTPUT OUT=MEAN_SAL (KEEP=GENDER M_SALARY)
          MEAN=M_SALARY;
RUN;

PROC SORT DATA=PAY1995;
   BY GENDER;
RUN;

DATA SAL_PER;
   MERGE PAY1995 MEAN_SAL;
   BY GENDER;
   PERCENT = 100*SALARY/M_SALARY;
DROP M_SALARY;
RUN;
```

```
PROC PRINT DATA=SAL_PER;
   TITLE 'Listing of Data Set SAL_PER';
RUN;
```

**SOLUTION TO PROBLEM 8**

```
*-------------------------------------------------------------*
| Create PAY1995 with code in PROBLEM 1                       |
*-------------------------------------------------------------*;
PROC MEANS DATA=PAY1995 NOPRINT;
   VAR SALARY;
   OUTPUT OUT=MEAN (KEEP=GRAND)
          MEAN=GRAND;
RUN;

DATA SAL_PER;
   SET PAY1995;
   IF _N_ = 1 THEN SET MEAN;
   PERCENT = 100*SALARY/GRAND;
   DROP GRAND;
RUN;

PROC PRINT DATA=SAL_PER;
   TITLE 'Listing of Data Set SAL_PER';
RUN;
```

**SOLUTION TO PROBLEM 9**

```
*-------------------------------------------------------------*
| Create PAY1995 with code in PROBLEM 1                       |
*-------------------------------------------------------------*;
DATA NEWDATA;
   LENGTH ID $ 3 GENDER $ 1;
   INPUT ID $ LEVEL SALARY GENDER;
DATALINES;
A23 . 72000 .
A24 36 77000 .
A13 . . M
;

PROC SORT DATA=PAY1995;
   BY ID;
RUN;

PROC SORT DATA=NEWDATA;
   BY ID;
RUN;

DATA PAY1995C;
   UPDATE PAY1995 NEWDATA;
   BY ID;
RUN;

PROC PRINT DATA=PAY1995C;
   TITLE 'Listing of Data Set PAY1995C';
RUN;
```

**SOLUTION TO PROBLEM 10**

```
*-------------------------------------------------------------*
| Create PAY1995 with code in PROBLEM 1                       |
*-------------------------------------------------------------*;
DATA BALL;
   INPUT ID : $3. HEIGHT;
```

```
DATALINES;
A24 65
A13 66
A23 72
;
PROC SORT DATA=BALL;
   BY ID;
RUN;

PROC SORT DATA=PAY1995;
   BY ID;
RUN;

DATA TEAM;
   MERGE PAY1995 (KEEP=ID GENDER)
         BALL  (IN=B_BALL);
   BY ID;
   IF B_BALL;
RUN;

PROC PRINT DATA=TEAM;
   TITLE 'Listing of Data Set TEAM';
RUN;
```

### SOLUTION TO PROBLEM 11

```
LIBNAME WORKBOOK 'C:\WORKBOOK';

*-------------------------------------------------------------*
| Create a data set of insurance allowance information        |
*-------------------------------------------------------------*;
DATA NEWINFO;
   INPUT GENDER : $1. LEVEL  : ALLOW COMMA5.;
DATALINES;
F 28 2,000
M 28 1,800
F 32 2,100
M 32 1,900
F 35 2,200
M 35 2,000
F 44 4,000
M 44 3,600
;
PROC SORT DATA=NEWINFO;
   BY GENDER LEVEL;
RUN;

PROC SORT DATA=PAY1995;
   BY GENDER LEVEL;
RUN;

DATA PAY1995H;
   MERGE PAY1995(IN=IN_PAY) NEWINFO;
   BY GENDER LEVEL;
   IF IN_PAY;
RUN;

PROC PRINT DATA=PAY1995H;
   TITLE 'Listing of Data Set PAY1995H';
RUN;
```

## SOLUTION TO PROBLEM 12

```
DATA TREAD;
   INPUT ID     $ 1-3
         MINUTES 5-6;
DATALINES;
123 10
811 12
586 14
278 11
193 12
;
DATA FAT;
   INPUT ID        $ 1-3
         BODY_FAT   5-6;
DATALINES;
444 14
123 23
919 18
278 20
444 24
811 34
193 30
;
PROC SORT DATA=TREAD;
   BY ID;
RUN;

PROC SORT DATA=FAT;
   BY ID;
RUN;

PROC SORT DATA=WORKBOOK.CLINICAL;
   BY ID;
RUN;

DATA STUDY;
   MERGE WORKBOOK.CLINICAL TREAD(IN=IN_TREAD) FAT(IN=IN_FAT);
   BY ID;
   IF IN_TREAD AND IN_FAT;
RUN;

PROC PRINT DATA=STUDY;
   TITLE 'Listing of Data Set STUDY';
RUN;
```

## SOLUTION TO PROBLEM 13

```
LIBNAME WORKBOOK 'C:\WORKBOOK';
OPTIONS FMTSEARCH=(WORKBOOK);

DATA TMP;
   SET WORKBOOK.CLINICAL(KEEP=GENDER DBP SBP DOB VISIT);
   AGE =  INT((VISIT - DOB) / 365.25);
   IF 0 LE AGE LE 30 THEN AGEGROUP = 1;
   ELSE IF 31 LE AGE LE 65 THEN AGEGROUP = 2;
   ELSE IF AGE GE 66 THEN AGEGROUP = 3;
   DROP AGE DOB VISIT;
RUN;

DATA TABLE;
   INPUT GENDER $ AGEGROUP D_LIMIT S_LIMIT;
```

```
DATALINES;
M 1 88 132
M 2 92 142
M 3 94 146
F 1 86 130
F 2 88 132
F 3 92 144
;

PROC SORT DATA=TMP;
   BY GENDER AGEGROUP;
RUN;

PROC SORT DATA=TABLE;
   BY GENDER AGEGROUP;
RUN;

DATA HYPERTEN;
   MERGE TMP(IN = IN_TMP) TABLE;
   BY GENDER AGEGROUP;
   IF IN_TMP;
   IF DBP GT D_LIMIT OR SBP GT S_LIMIT THEN HYPER = 'Y';
   ELSE IF DBP NE . AND SBP NE .       THEN HYPER = 'N';
   DROP D_LIMIT S_LIMIT AGEGROUP;
RUN;

PROC PRINT DATA=HYPERTEN;
   TITLE 'Listing of Data Set HYPERTEN';
RUN;
```

# CHAPTER 5 Using Numerical Functions

## SOLUTION TO PROBLEM 1

```
DATA XYZ;
   INPUT X Y Z;
   ROUND_X = ROUND(X,.1);
   LOG_X = LOG(X);
   LOG10_X = LOG10(X);
   WHOLE_X = INT(X);
   SMALL = MIN(OF X Y Z);
   BIG = MAX(OF X Y Z);
   AVE = MEAN(OF X Y Z);
   SUM = SUM(OF X Y Z);
   NONMISS = N(OF X Y Z);
DATALINES;
1 2 3
4 . 6
2.33 5 .
2.5 2.6 2.7
;
PROC PRINT DATA=XYZ;
   TITLE 'Listing of Data Set XYZ';
RUN;
```

## SOLUTION TO PROBLEM 2

```
DATA WHOLE;
   DO SUBJECT = 1 TO 12;
    ***Generate uniform random numbers from 1 to 100;
      SCORE = INT(100 * RANUNI(0) + 1);
      OUTPUT;
   END;
RUN;

DATA EVERY3RD;
   SET WHOLE;
   IF MOD(_N_,3)=1;
RUN;

PROC PRINT DATA=EVERY3RD;
   TITLE 'Listing of Data Set EVERY3RD';
RUN;
```

## SOLUTION TO PROBLEM 3

```
DATA MOVING;
   LENGTH MONTH $ 3; ***Optional statement;
   INPUT MONTH $ COST;
   COST1 = LAG(COST);
   COST2 = LAG2(COST);
   IF _N_ GE 3 THEN MOVE_AVE = MEAN(OF COST COST1 COST2);
DATALINES;
JAN       125
FEB       120
MAR       130
APR       100
MAY       140
JUN       180
JUL       200
;
PROC PRINT DATA=MOVING;
   TITLE 'Listing of Data Set MOVING';
RUN;
```

**SOLUTION TO PROBLEM 4**

```
DATA SURVEY;
   INPUT ID QUES1-QUES10;
   IF N(OF QUES1-QUES10) GE 8 THEN SCORE = MEAN(OF QUES1-QUES10);
DATALINES;
1    3    4    3    2    .    5    5    4    4    3
2    .    .    .    2    1    1    1    2    1    2
3    5    4    5    3    3    4    5    4    .    5
;
PROC PRINT DATA=SURVEY;
   TITLE 'Listing of Data Set SURVEY';
RUN;
```

**SOLUTION TO PROBLEM 5**

```
DATA NEW;
   SET WHOLE; ***From Problem 2;
***Part A;
   DIFF1 = DIF(SCORE);
   ***You could also use the LAG function and then compute a
      difference;
***Part B;
   DIFF2 = DIF2(SCORE);
RUN;

PROC PRINT DATA=NEW;
   TITLE 'Listing of Data Set NEW';
RUN;
```

**SOLUTION TO PROBLEM 6**

```
DATA MULTIPLE;
   INPUT SUBJECT 1-2 X 4 Y 6 Z 8;
DATALINES;
01 1 2 3
01 4 5 6
01 7 8 9
02 8 7 6
02 5 4 3
02 2 1 0
;
PROC SORT DATA=MULTIPLE;
   BY SUBJECT;
RUN;

DATA ONE;
   SET MULTIPLE;
   BY SUBJECT;

   *-------------------------------------------------------------*
   | The difference variables and mean scores in the lines that  |
   | follow are correct only when you reach the third observation |
   | for each ID.  However, you must execute the DIF functions   |
   | for each observation for the program to work.  The key is to |
   | output an observation only when you are processing the last |
   | (third) observation for each ID.                             |
   *-------------------------------------------------------------*;
   DIF_X23 = DIF(X);
   DIF_Y23 = DIF(Y);
   DIF_Z23 = DIF(Z);
   DIF_X13 = DIF2(X);
   DIF_Y13 = DIF2(Y);
   DIF_Z13 = DIF2(Z);
```

```
   MEAN_X  = (X + LAG(X) + LAG2(X))/3;
   MEAN_Y  = (Y + LAG(Y) + LAG2(Y))/3;
   MEAN_Z  = (Z + LAG(Z) + LAG2(Z))/3;
   IF LAST.SUBJECT;
RUN;

PROC PRINT DATA=ONE;
   TITLE 'Listing of Data Set ONE';
RUN;
```

**SOLUTION TO PROBLEM 7**

```
DATA CHAR;
   INPUT AGE $ HEIGHT $ WEIGHT $;
DATALINES;
23 68 160
44 72 200
55  . 180
;
DATA NUM;
   SET CHAR (RENAME=(AGE=CAGE
                     HEIGHT=CHEIGHT
                     WEIGHT=CWEIGHT));
   AGE = INPUT(CAGE,5.);
   HEIGHT = INPUT(CHEIGHT,5.);
   WEIGHT = INPUT(CWEIGHT,5.);
   DROP CAGE CHEIGHT CWEIGHT;
RUN;

PROC PRINT DATA=NUM;
   TITLE 'Listing of Data Set NUM';
RUN;
```

**SOLUTION TO PROBLEM 8**

```
DATA TRIG;
   INPUT DEGREE RADIAN SINE COSINE TANGENT;
   PI = 3.14159; ***Alternative:  RETAIN PI 3.14159;

   *------------------------------------------------------------*
   | Another alternative is to use one of the trig functions    |
   | to compute a value for PI (which is then retained) such    |
   | as:                                                        |
   | RETAIN PI;                                                 |
   | IF _N_ = 1 THEN PI = ARCOS(-1);                            |
   *------------------------------------------------------------*;
   ANGLE_R = PI*DEGREE/180;
   SIN_DEG = SIN(ANGLE_R);
   COS_DEG = COS(ANGLE_R);
   TAN_DEG = TAN(ANGLE_R);
   SIN_RAD = SIN(RADIAN);
   COS_RAD = COS(RADIAN);
   TAN_RAD = TAN(RADIAN);
   ANGLES_D = 180*ARSIN(SINE)/PI;
   ANGLES_R = ARSIN(SINE);
   ANGLEC_D = 180*ARCOS(COSINE)/PI;
   ANGLEC_R = ARCOS(COSINE);
   ANGLET_D = 180*ATAN(TANGENT)/PI;
   ANGLET_R = ATAN(TANGENT);

***The labels are optional;
   LABEL ANGLE_R = 'Angle in radians'
      SIN_DEG = 'Sine of degree'
      COS_DEG = 'Cosine of degree'
```

```
        TAN_DEG = 'Tangent of degree'
        SIN_RAD = 'Sine of radian'
        COS_RAD = 'Cosine of radian'
        TAN_RAD = 'Tangent of radian'
        ANGLES_D = 'Arcsine of SINE in degrees'
        ANGLES_R = 'Arcsine of SINE in radians'
        ANGLEC_D = 'Arcosine of COSINE in degrees'
        ANGLEC_R = 'Arcosine of COSINE in radians'
        ANGLET_D = 'Arctangent of TANGENT in degrees'
        ANGLET_R = 'Arctangent of TANGENT in radians';
DATALINES;
  30      1       .5     .5      .5
  45   3.14159   1       1       1
   0   .5708    .707   .707     0
 390     10      .003   .003    .003
;
PROC PRINT DATA=TRIG;
   TITLE 'Listing of Data Set TRIG';
RUN;
```

### SOLUTION TO PROBLEM 9

```
*-------------------------------------------------------------*
| The more elegant solution to this problem (suggested by     |
| one of my students and one of the reviewers) is shown here. |
| In it, the lowest score is identified and subtracted from   |
| the sum of scores which, in turn, is divided by n-1 or 4.   |
*-------------------------------------------------------------*;
DATA GRADES;
   ARRAY QUIZ[5];
   INPUT STUDENT $ QUIZ1-QUIZ5;
   LOW = MIN(OF QUIZ1-QUIZ5);
   IF N(OF QUIZ1-QUIZ5) = 5 THEN
      QUIZ_AVE = (SUM(OF QUIZ1-QUIZ5) - LOW) / 4;
   ELSE QUIZ_AVE = MEAN(OF QUIZ[*]);
   ***Alternate line: QUIZ_AVE = MEAN(OF QUIZ1-QUIZ5);
   DROP LOW;
DATALINES;
Baggett    4       2       6       2       3
Ginn       9       9      10       .       9
Cody      10      10       9      10      10
Smith      .       .       2       3       4
;
PROC PRINT DATA=GRADES;
   TITLE 'Listing of Data Set GRADES';
   ID STUDENT;
   VAR QUIZ1-QUIZ5 QUIZ_AVE;
RUN;

 /*------------------------------------------------------------*
  | Alternate Solution: A more "brute force" approach in       |
  | which the lowest score is identified and the corresponding |
  | quiz score is set to missing. (Also called a "brut force"  |
  | approach but, so much for my "dry" humor.)                 |
  |                                                            |
  | DATA GRADES;                                               |
  |    ARRAY QUIZ[5];                                          |
  |    INPUT STUDENT $ QUIZ1-QUIZ5;                            |
  |    LOW = MIN(OF QUIZ1-QUIZ5);                              |
  |    IF N(OF QUIZ1-QUIZ5) = 5 THEN DO I = 1 TO 5;            |
  |       IF QUIZ[I]=LOW THEN DO;                              |
  |          QUIZ[I] = .;                                      |
```

```
|         LEAVE; ***Notice this useful statement;                |
|      END;                                                      |
|   END;                                                         |
|                                                                |
| QUIZ_AVE = MEAN(OF QUIZ[*]);                                   |
| ***Alternate line: QUIZ_AVE = MEAN(OF QUIZ1-QUIZ5);            |
| DROP I LOW;                                                    |
| DATALINES;                                                     |
| Baggett    4       2       6       2       3                    |
| Ginn       9       9      10       .       9                    |
| Cody      10      10       9      10      10                    |
| Smith      .       .       2       3       4                    |
| ;                                                              |
| PROC PRINT DATA=GRADES;                                        |
|    TITLE 'Listing of Data Set GRADES';                         |
|    ID STUDENT;                                                 |
|    VAR QUIZ1-QUIZ5 QUIZ_AVE;                                   |
| RUN;                                                           |
|                                                                |
*----------------------------------------------------------------*/
```

# CHAPTER 6 Using Character Functions

## SOLUTION TO PROBLEM 1

```
DATA TEMP_FC;
   LENGTH DUMMY $ 4 NUMBER $ 3 LETTER $ 1;
   INPUT DUMMY $ @@;
   ***Separate number and letter parts;
   LEN = LENGTH (DUMMY);
   NUMBER = SUBSTR(DUMMY,1,LEN-1);
   LETTER = SUBSTR(DUMMY,LEN,1);
   IF LETTER = 'F' THEN TEMP = (INPUT(NUMBER,3.)-32)*5/9;
   ELSE TEMP = INPUT(NUMBER,3.);
   KEEP TEMP;
DATALINES;
32F  42C  137F  84F  20C
;
PROC PRINT;
   TITLE 'Listing of Data Set TEMP_FC';
RUN;

 /*------------------------------------------------------------*
   | Here is an interesting alternative program which uses      |
   | other string functions.                                    |
   |                                                            |
   | DATA TEMP_FC;                                              |
   |    LENGTH DUMMY $ 4;                                       |
   |    INPUT DUMMY $ @@;                                       |
   |  ***Extract the number part by eliminating the C's and F's |
   |  ***and perform a character to numeric conversion.;        |
   |     TEMP = INPUT (COMPRESS(DUMMY,'FC'),3.);                |
   |  ***Check if original value had a C or F;                  |
   |       IF INDEX(DUMMY,'F') GT 0 THEN TEMP = (TEMP-32)*5/9;  |
   | KEEP TEMP;                                                 |
   | DATALINES;                                                 |
   | 32F  42C  137F  84F  20C                                   |
   | ;                                                          |
   | PROC PRINT;                                                |
   |    TITLE 'Listing of Data Set TEMP_FC (Alt. Method)';      |
   | RUN;                                                       |
  *------------------------------------------------------------*/
```

## SOLUTION TO PROBLEM 2

```
DATA INVALID;
   INPUT @1  ID     $3.
         @4  STRING $10.;
   IF VERIFY (STRING,'ABCDE ') NE 0 THEN OUTPUT;
DATALINES;
001ABCDEABCDE
002XCCBEBBABC
003A BACECBAA
004abcdeabcde
;
PROC PRINT;
   TITLE 'Listing of Data Set INVALID';
RUN;
```

## SOLUTION TO PROBLEM 3

```
DATA PACK;
   INPUT TEN $10.;
DATALINES;
0123456789
```

```
1 2 3 4 56
3428645889
;
DATA UNPACK;
   SET PACK;
   ARRAY X[10] X1-X10;
   DO J = 1 TO 10;
      X[J] = INPUT(SUBSTR(TEN,J,1),1.);
   END;
DROP J TEN;
RUN;

PROC PRINT DATA=UNPACK;
   TITLE 'Listing of Data Set UNPACK';
RUN;
```

## SOLUTION TO PROBLEM 4

```
DATA CONVERT;
   ARRAY Q[5] $ 1 Q1-Q5;
   INPUT @1 (Q1-Q5)($1.);
   DO I = 1 TO 5;
      Q[I] = TRANSLATE(Q[I],'ABCDE','12345');
   END;
   DROP I;
DATALINES;
12345
3 414
54321
;
PROC PRINT DATA=CONVERT;
   TITLE 'Listing of Data Set CONVERT';
RUN;
```

## SOLUTION TO PROBLEM 5

```
DATA TEST;
   RETAIN CHECK 'ABCDE '; ***Alternative: CHECK = 'ABCDE ';
   INPUT (QUES1-QUES5)($1.);
   ARRAY QUES[5] $ 1 QUES1-QUES5;
   DO I = 1 TO 5;
      QUES[I] = UPCASE(QUES[I]);
      QUES[I] = TRANSLATE (QUES[I],'ABCDE','12345');
      IF VERIFY (QUES[I],CHECK) GT 0 THEN QUES[I] = ' ';
   END;
   DROP I;
DATALINES;
12345
aBcDe
xY73E
3 E w
;
PROC PRINT DATA=TEST;
   TITLE 'Listing of Data set TEST';
   VAR QUES1-QUES5;
RUN;
```

## SOLUTION TO PROBLEM 6

```
*-----------------------------------------------------------*
| Program to encode a message                               |
*-----------------------------------------------------------*;
DATA _NULL_;
   FILE PRINT;
   INPUT LINE $80.;
```

```
   TOSTRING = 'QWERTYUIOPLKJHGFDSAZXCVBNM';
   FRSTRING = 'ABCDEFGHIJKLMNOPQRSTUVWXYZ';
   LINE = UPCASE(LINE);
   ENCODE = TRANSLATE(LINE,TOSTRING,FRSTRING);
   PUT ENCODE;
DATALINES;
This is a TEST
Line TWO of the Message
;
RUN;
```

## SOLUTION TO PROBLEM 7

```
*---------------------------------------------------------------*
| Program to decode a message                                   |
*---------------------------------------------------------------*;
DATA _NULL_;
   FILE PRINT;
   INPUT LINE $80.;
   TOSTRING = 'ABCDEFGHIJKLMNOPQRSTUVWXYZ';
   FRSTRING = 'QWERTYUIOPLKJHGFDSAZXCVBNM';
   DECODE = TRANSLATE(LINE,TOSTRING,FRSTRING);
   PUT DECODE;
DATALINES;
ZIOA OA Q ZTAZ
KOHT ZVG GY ZIT JTAAQUT
;
RUN;
```

# CHAPTER 7 Working with Dates

### SOLUTION TO PROBLEM 1

```
DATA IN_DATE;
   INPUT @1  DATE1  MMDDYY6.
         @8  DATE2  MMDDYY8.
         @17 DATE3  DATE7.
         @25 DATE4  JULIAN5.
         @31 DATE5  DDMMYY6.
         @38 DATE6  MMDDYY8.;
   FORMAT DATE1-DATE6 MMDDYY8.;
DATALINES;
102146 10/21/46 21OCT46 46294 211046 10211946
122596 12/25/96 25DEC96 96360 251296 12251996
;
PROC PRINT DATA=IN_DATE;
   TITLE 'Listing of Data Set IN_DATE';
RUN;
```

### SOLUTION TO PROBLEM 2

```
DATA IN_DATE2;
   INPUT DAY1    3-4
         MONTH1 10-11
         YEAR1  15-18
         MONTH2 20-21
         YEAR2  23-24;
   DATE1 = MDY(MONTH1,DAY1,YEAR1);
   DATE2 = MDY(MONTH2,15,YEAR2);
   TIMESPAN = ROUND ((DATE2 - DATE1)/365.25,1);
   FORMAT DATE1 DATE2 WORDDATE.;
   KEEP DATE1 DATE2 TIMESPAN;
DATALINES;
  17     09    1990 04 96
  30     11    1991 05 95
;
PROC PRINT DATA=IN_DATE2;
   TITLE 'Listing of Data Set IN_DATE2';
RUN;
```

### SOLUTION TO PROBLEM 3

```
LIBNAME WORKBOOK 'C:\WORKBOOK';
OPTIONS FMTSEARCH=(WORKBOOK);

DATA AGE;
   SET WORKBOOK.CLINICAL(KEEP=ID DOB VISIT);
   AGE1 = ROUND(('01JAN96'D - DOB)/365.25);
   AGE2 = INT((VISIT - DOB)/365.25);
   AGE3 = ROUND((TODAY() - DOB)/365.25,.5);
RUN;

PROC PRINT DATA=AGE;
   TITLE 'Listing of Data Set AGE';
RUN;
```

### SOLUTION TO PROBLEM 4

```
LIBNAME WORKBOOK 'C:\WORKBOOK';
OPTIONS FMTSEARCH=(WORKBOOK);

PROC FORMAT;
   VALUE DAYWK 1 = 'Mon'  2 = 'Tue'  3 = 'Wed'  4 = 'Thu'
               5 = 'Fri'  6 = 'Sat'  7 = 'Sun';
```

```
   VALUE MON   1  = 'Jan'  2  = 'Feb'  3  = 'Mar'  4  = 'Apr'
               5  = 'May'  6  = 'Jun'  7  = 'Jul'  8  = 'Aug'
               9  = 'Sep' 10  = 'Oct' 11  = 'Nov' 12  = 'Dec';
RUN;

DATA CLINDATE;
   SET WORKBOOK.CLINICAL(KEEP=ID VISIT);
   DAY_WEEK = WEEKDAY(VISIT);
   MONTH = MONTH(VISIT);
   YEAR = YEAR(VISIT);
   FORMAT DAY_WEEK DAYWK.
          MONTH    MON.;
RUN;

PROC FREQ DATA=CLINDATE;
   TITLE 'Frequencies from CLINDATE';
   TABLES DAY_WEEK MONTH YEAR / NOCUM;
RUN;
```

**SOLUTION TO PROBLEM 5**

```
LIBNAME WORKBOOK 'C:\WORKBOOK';
OPTIONS FMTSEARCH=(WORKBOOK);

DATA CLINDATE;
   SET WORKBOOK.CLINICAL(KEEP=ID VISIT);
   DAY_WEEK = PUT(VISIT,WEEKDATE3.);
   MONTH = PUT(VISIT,MONNAME3.);
   YEAR = YEAR(VISIT);
RUN;

PROC FREQ DATA=CLINDATE;
   TITLE 'Frequencies from CLINDATE';
   TABLES DAY_WEEK MONTH / NOCUM;
RUN;
```

# CHAPTER 8 Using Arrays

## SOLUTION TO PROBLEM 1

```
DATA LOTS_9;
   INPUT X1-X5 A B C D Y1-Y5 Z1-Z3;
DATALINES;
1 0 1 0 1 2 2 2 2 1 2 3 4 5 3 3 3
9 0 0 0 9 99 99 99 7 999 999 4 5 6 999 999 999
;

DATA LOTSMISS;
   SET LOTS_9;
   ARRAY X9[5] X1-X5;
   ARRAY X99[4] A B C D;
   ARRAY X999[8] Y1-Y5 Z1-Z3;

*-------------------------------------------------------------*
| Since there are different numbers of elements in each of     |
| these arrays, you can either have separate loops for each    |
| or place a test inside a loop which goes from 1 to 8.        |
*-------------------------------------------------------------*;
   DO I = 1 TO 8;
      IF I LE 5 AND   X9[I] = 9   THEN   X9[I] = .;
      IF I LE 4 AND  X99[I] = 99  THEN  X99[I] = .;
      IF            X999[I] = 999 THEN X999[I] = .;
   END;

   DROP I;
RUN;

PROC PRINT DATA=LOTSMISS;
   TITLE 'Listing of Data Set LOTSMISS';
RUN;
```

## SOLUTION TO PROBLEM 2

```
DATA NOTAPPLY;
   LENGTH A B C D E $ 2;
   INPUT ID A $ B $ C $ D $ E $ X Y Z;
DATALINES;
001 Y N N Y Y 1 2 3
002 na NA Y Y Y 3 4 5
003 NA NA NA na na 8 9 10
;

DATA NEW;
   SET NOTAPPLY;
   ARRAY PRESTON[*] _CHARACTER_; ***Yes, Preston is a character!;

   DO I = 1 TO DIM(PRESTON);
      IF UPCASE(PRESTON[I]) = 'NA' THEN PRESTON[I] = ' ';
   END;

   DROP I;
RUN;

PROC PRINT DATA=NEW;
   TITLE 'Listing of Data Set NEW';
RUN;
```

## SOLUTION TO PROBLEM 3

```
DATA TEMPER;
   ARRAY F[30]; ***Short hand for ARRAY F[30] F1-F30;

   DO OBS = 1 TO 5;
      DO I = 1 TO 30;
         ***The line below will randomly generate temperatures
            from 32 to 212;
         F[I] = INT(RANUNI(0)*181 + 32);
      END;
      OUTPUT;
   END;

   KEEP F1-F30;
RUN;

DATA TEMPER2;
   SET TEMPER;
   ARRAY C[30]; *** Or ARRAY C[30] C1-C30;
   ARRAY F[30]; *** Or ARRAY F[30] F1-F30;


   DO I = 1 TO 30;
      C[I] = 5*(F[I] - 32)/9;
   END;

   DROP I F1-F30;
RUN;

PROC PRINT DATA=TEMPER2;
   TITLE 'Listing of Data Set TEMPER2';
RUN;
```

## SOLUTION TO PROBLEM 4

```
DATA DIAG;
   INFILE DATALINES PAD;
   INPUT @1  ID $3.
         @5 (DX1-DX5)($2. + 1);
DATALINES;
001 11 12
002 01 02 03 04 05
003 12
004 05 06
005 AA BB CC DD EE
;

DATA DIAG2;
   SET DIAG;
   ARRAY D[5] $ DX1-DX5;

   DO I = 1 TO 5;
      DX = D[I];
      IF DX NE ' ' THEN OUTPUT;
   END;

   KEEP ID DX;
RUN;

PROC PRINT DATA=DIAG2;
   TITLE 'Listing of Data Set DIAG2';
RUN;
```

### SOLUTION TO PROBLEM 5

```
DATA MANY;
   INPUT ID TIME X Y Z;
DATALINES;
1    1     1    2    3
1    2     4    5    6
1    3     7    8    9
2    1    10   20   30
2    3    40    .   50
3    1    15    .    .
3    2    25   26   27
3    3    35   36   37
;

PROC SORT DATA=MANY;
   ***Data set does not have to be in TIME order;
   BY ID;
RUN;

DATA ONEPER;
   RETAIN X1-X3 Y1-Y3 Z1-Z3;
   ARRAY XX[3] X1-X3;
   ARRAY YY[3] Y1-Y3;
   ARRAY ZZ[3] Z1-Z3;
   SET MANY;
      BY ID;

*-------------------------------------------------------------*
| Initialize all variables to missing if this is the first     |
| observation for a subject.  Otherwise, if a subject is       |
| missing an observation for one or more times, that subject   |
| will be given the values from the previous subject           |
*-------------------------------------------------------------*;
   IF FIRST.ID THEN DO I = 1 TO 3;
      XX[I] = .;
      YY[I] = .;
      ZZ[I] = .;
   END;

   XX[TIME] = X;
   YY[TIME] = Y;
   ZZ[TIME] = Z;

   IF LAST.ID THEN OUTPUT;


   KEEP ID X1-X3 Y1-Y3 Z1-Z3;
RUN;

PROC PRINT DATA=ONEPER;
   TITLE 'Listing of Data Set ONEPER';
RUN;
```

### SOLUTION TO PROBLEM 6

```
DATA PAYROLL;
   INPUT AMT1990-AMT1996;
DATALINES;
50000 55000 57000 62000 66000 70000 72000
40000 43000 44000 55000 65000 69000 73000
;
```

```
DATA TAXES;
   SET PAYROLL;
   ARRAY AMT[1990:1996] AMT1990-AMT1996;
   ARRAY TAX[1990:1996] TAX1990-TAX1996;

   DO I = 1990 TO 1996;
   ***Alternate: DO I = LBOUND(AMT) TO UBOUND(AMT);
      TAX[I] = AMT[I] * .25;
   END;

   FORMAT AMT1990-AMT1996  TAX1990-TAX1996 DOLLAR9.0;
   DROP I;
RUN;

PROC PRINT DATA=TAXES;
   TITLE 'Listing of Data Set TAXES';
RUN;
```

## SOLUTION TO PROBLEM 7

```
DATA SCORE;
   ARRAY PASS[5] _TEMPORARY_ (65 70 65 60 75);
   ARRAY TEST[5] TEST1-TEST5;
   INPUT STUDENT $ TEST1-TEST5;
   NUM_PASS = 0;
   DO I = 1 TO 5;
      IF TEST[I] GE PASS[I] THEN NUM_PASS + 1;
   END;

 /*-----------------------------------------------*
  | Alternate code: A bit more elegant            |
  | DO I = 1 TO 5;                                |
  |    NUM_PASS + (TEST[I] GE PASS[I]);           |
  | END;                                          |
  *-----------------------------------------------*/

   DROP I;
DATALINES;
Bob         45     68     80     65     60
Michelle    80     90     95     90     87
Clifton     59     69     79     89     99
;

PROC PRINT DATA=SCORE;
   TITLE 'Listing of Data Set SCORE';
RUN;
```

# CHAPTER 9 Looking Back and Ahead Across Observations

## SOLUTION TO PROBLEM 1

```
DATA INITIAL;
   INFILE 'C:\WORKBOOK\DIALYSIS.DTA' PAD;
   INPUT @1  ID     $3.
         @4  GENDER $1.
         @5  DOB    MMDDYY8.
         @13 VISIT  1.
         @14 HR     3.
         @17 SBP    3.
         @20 DBP    3.;
   FORMAT DOB MMDDYY8.;
DATALINES;
001M10/21/461080140080
001         2082142084
001         3078138078
002F11/17/221066120070
003F04/04/181084150090
003         2088152102
004M12/21/101072120074
004         2070122076
004         3078128078
005F08/02/311092180110
006         1076180112
006         2080178090
;

PROC SORT DATA=INITIAL;
   BY ID;
RUN;

DATA DIALYSIS;
   SET INITIAL;
   BY ID;
   RETAIN OLDGEND OLDDOB;
   IF FIRST.ID THEN DO;
      OLDGEND = GENDER;
      OLDDOB =  DOB;
   END;
   ELSE DO;
      GENDER = OLDGEND;
      DOB = OLDDOB;
   END;
   DROP OLDGEND OLDDOB;
RUN;

PROC PRINT DATA=DIALYSIS;
   TITLE 'Listing of Data Set DIALYSIS';
RUN;
```

## SOLUTION TO PROBLEM 2

```
DATA STOCKS;
   INPUT DATE : MMDDYY8. PRICE;
   MOVE_AVE = (PRICE + LAG(PRICE) + LAG2(PRICE))/3;
   IF _N_ LT 3 THEN MOVE_AVE = .;
   ***Be sure not to conditionally execute the LAG functions;
   FORMAT DATE MMDDYY8. PRICE MOVE_AVE DOLLAR8.;
DATALINES;
01/01/95    23.00
01/02/95    25.00
```

```
01/03/95    24.00
01/04/95    29.00
01/05/95    26.00
01/06/95    23.00
01/07/95    24.00
;

PROC PRINT DATA=STOCKS;
   TITLE 'Listing of Data Set STOCKS';
RUN;

PROC PLOT DATA=STOCKS;
   TITLE1 'Plot of Daily Prices and Moving Averages';
   TITLE2 'o Represent Daily Prices, - Represent a Moving Average';
   PLOT PRICE * DATE = 'o'  MOVE_AVE * DATE = '-' / OVERLAY;
RUN;
```

**SOLUTION TO PROBLEM 3**

```
*-------------------------------------------------------------*
| This solution is not very elegant but gets the job done.    |
*-------------------------------------------------------------*;
DATA OK NOT_OK;
   INPUT ID : $1. TRIAL X Y Z;
   ID2 = LAG(ID);
   ID3 = LAG2(ID);
   X2 = LAG(X);  Y2=LAG(Y);  Z2=LAG(Z);
   X3 = LAG2(X); Y3=LAG2(Y); Z3=LAG2(Z);

   IF TRIAL = 3 THEN DO;
      IF (ID = ID2) AND (ID = ID3) THEN DO;
         OUTPUT OK;
         TRIAL = 1; ID = ID3; X = X3; Y = Y3; Z = Z3;
         OUTPUT OK;
         TRIAL = 2; ID = ID2; X = X2; Y = Y2; Z = Z2;
         OUTPUT OK;
      END;
      ELSE DO;
         OUTPUT NOT_OK;
         TRIAL = 1; ID = ID3; X = X3; Y = Y3; Z = Z3;
         OUTPUT NOT_OK;
         TRIAL = 2; ID = ID2; X = X2; Y = Y2; Z = Z2;
         OUTPUT NOT_OK;
      END;
   END;

   KEEP ID TRIAL X Y Z;
DATALINES;
1     1     1    2    3
1     2     2    3    6
1     3     4    1    2
2     1     4    5    6
9     2     5    4    3
2     3     1    2    1
3     1     2    2    2
3     2     3    3    3
3     3     4    5    6
;

 /*------------------------------------------------------------*
  | This alternate solution is still not very elegant but it   |
  | is a little shorter than the solution above.               |
  |                                                            |
```

```
| DATA OK NOT_OK;                                            |
|    INPUT ID : $1. TRIAL X Y Z;                             |
|    ID2 = LAG(ID);                                          |
|    ID3 = LAG2(ID);                                         |
|    X2 = LAG(X);  Y2=LAG(Y);  Z2=LAG(Z);                    |
|    X3 = LAG2(X); Y3=LAG2(Y); Z3=LAG2(Z);                   |
|                                                            |
|    IF TRIAL = 3 THEN DO;                                   |
|       IF (ID = ID2) AND (ID = ID3) THEN OK = 'Y';          |
|       ELSE OK='N';                                         |
|       IF OK='Y' THEN OUTPUT OK;                            |
|       ELSE OUTPUT NOT_OK;                                  |
|       TRIAL = 1; ID = ID3; X = X3; Y = Y3; Z = Z3;         |
|       IF OK='Y' THEN OUTPUT OK;                            |
|       ELSE OUTPUT NOT_OK;                                  |
|       TRIAL = 2; ID = ID2; X = X2; Y = Y2; Z = Z2;         |
|       IF OK='Y' THEN OUTPUT OK;                            |
|       ELSE OUTPUT NOT_OK;                                  |
|    END;                                                    |
|                                                            |
|    KEEP ID TRIAL X Y Z;                                    |
| DATALINES;                                                 |
*------------------------------------------------------------*/

PROC PRINT DATA=OK;
   TITLE 'Listing of Data Set OK';
RUN;

PROC PRINT DATA=NOT_OK;
   TITLE 'Listing of Data Set NOT_OK';
RUN;
```

**SOLUTION TO PROBLEM 4**

```
DATA STREP;
   INPUT @1  ID     $1.
         @3  VISIT  MMDDYY8.
         @12 DOCTOR $3.;
   FORMAT VISIT MMDDYY8.;
DATALINES;
1 11/01/95 ABC
1 12/01/95 XYZ
2 12/01/95 JBD
2 12/07/95 RPC
3 01/05/96 ABC
3 05/05/96 JBD
3 07/01/96 XYZ

;
DATA BLAME;
   SET STREP;
   SET STREP(FIRSTOBS=2
             RENAME=(VISIT=NEXTDATE ID=NEXTID)
             DROP=DOCTOR);
   DIFF = NEXTDATE - VISIT;
   IF ID = NEXTID THEN DO;
      IF DIFF LE 90 THEN OUTCOME = 'FAILURE';
      ELSE OUTCOME = 'SUCCESS';
   END;
   ELSE OUTCOME = 'SUCCESS';
   KEEP ID VISIT DOCTOR OUTCOME;
RUN;
```

```
PROC PRINT DATA=BLAME;
   TITLE 'Listing of Data Set BLAME';
RUN;
```

# CHAPTER 10 Working with Longitudinal Data: Multiple Observations per Subject

## SOLUTION TO PROBLEM 1

```
***The formats below are optional;
PROC FORMAT;
   VALUE $DXCODES '01' = 'Cold'
                  '02' = 'Flu'
                  '03' = 'Break/Fracture'
                  '04' = 'Routine Physical'
                  '05' = 'Heart Problem'
                  '06' = 'Lung Disorder'
                  '07' = 'Abdominal Pain'
                  '08' = 'Laceration'
                  '09' = 'Resp. Infection'
                  '10' = 'Lyme disease'
                  '11' = 'Ear Ache';
   VALUE $RXCODES  '1' = 'Immunization'
                   '2' = 'Casting'
                   '3' = 'Beta Blocker'
                   '4' = 'ACE Inhibitor'
                   '5' = 'Antihistamine'
                   '6' = 'Ibuprofen'
                   '7' = 'Aspirin'
                   '8' = 'Antibiotic';
RUN;

DATA CLIN_X;
   INFILE 'C:\WORKBOOK\CLIN_X.DTA' PAD;
   INPUT   @1  ID      $3.
           @4  VISIT    MMDDYY6.
           @10 DX      $2.
           @12 HR       3.
           @15 SBP      3.
           @18 DBP      3.
           RX_1        $1.
           RX_2        $1.;
FORMAT VISIT MMDDYY8.
       DX $DXCODES.
       RX_1 RX_2 $RXCODES.;
RUN;


PROC SORT DATA=CLIN_X;
   BY ID VISIT;
RUN;

DATA FIRST LAST; ***Note: You can create both data sets
                          in one DATA step;
   SET CLIN_X;
   BY ID;
   IF FIRST.ID THEN OUTPUT FIRST;
   IF LAST.ID THEN OUTPUT LAST;
*-------------------------------------------------------------*
| Do not use an IF-THEN/ELSE here since you want patients     |
| with a single visit to be in both data sets.                |
*-------------------------------------------------------------*;
RUN;

PROC PRINT DATA=FIRST;
   TITLE 'Listing of data set FIRST';
RUN;
```

```
PROC PRINT DATA=LAST;
   TITLE 'Listing of data set LAST';
RUN;
```

**SOLUTION TO PROBLEM 2**

```
*-------------------------------------------------------------*
| Create and sort data set CLIN_X as in PROBLEM 1.            |
*-------------------------------------------------------------*;

*-------------------------------------------------------------*
| Data set COUNT contains the IDs for all patients with       |
| 4 visits.                                                   |
*-------------------------------------------------------------*;
DATA COUNT;
   SET CLIN_X (KEEP=ID);
   BY ID;
   IF FIRST.ID THEN N=1;
   ELSE N+1;
   IF LAST.ID AND N=4 THEN OUTPUT;
   DROP N;
RUN;


DATA FOUR;
   MERGE CLIN_X COUNT (IN=ONLY4);
   BY ID;
   IF ONLY4;
RUN;

PROC PRINT DATA=FOUR;
   TITLE 'Listing of data set FOUR';
RUN;
```

**SOLUTION TO PROBLEM 3**

```
*-------------------------------------------------------------*
| Create and sort data set CLIN_X as in PROBLEM 1.            |
*-------------------------------------------------------------*;
PROC FREQ DATA=CLIN_X;
   TABLES ID / NOPRINT OUT=COUNTER (KEEP=ID COUNT);
RUN;

DATA FOUR;
   MERGE CLIN_X COUNTER (IN=ONLY4
                         WHERE=(COUNT=4));
   BY ID;
   IF ONLY4;
   DROP COUNT;
RUN;

 /*---------------------------------------------------*
  | Alternative:                                      |
  |                                                   |
  | DATA FOUR;                                        |
  |    MERGE CLIN_X COUNTER (IN=ONLY4);               |
  |    BY ID;                                         |
  |    IF ONLY4 AND COUNT=4;                          |
  |    DROP COUNT;                                    |
  | RUN;                                              |
  *---------------------------------------------------*/
```

```
PROC PRINT DATA=FOUR;
   TITLE 'Listing of data set FOUR';
RUN;
```

**SOLUTION TO PROBLEM 4**

```
DATA MISSING;
   INFILE 'C:\WORKBOOK\BASKETBA.DTA' PAD;
   INPUT @1  ID      $3.
         @5  GENDER  $1.
         @7  HEIGHT   2.
         @10 DATE    MMDDYY8.
         @19 POINTS   2.;
   FORMAT DATE MMDDYY8.;
RUN;

PROC SORT DATA=MISSING;
   BY ID;
RUN;

DATA BASKET;
   SET MISSING;
   BY ID;
   RETAIN H_GENDER H_HEIGHT;
   IF FIRST.ID THEN DO;
      H_GENDER = GENDER;
      H_HEIGHT = HEIGHT;
   END;
   ELSE DO;
      GENDER = H_GENDER;
      HEIGHT = H_HEIGHT;
   END;
DROP H_GENDER H_HEIGHT;
RUN;

PROC PRINT DATA=BASKET;
   TITLE 'Listing of data set BASKET';
RUN;
```

**SOLUTION TO PROBLEM 5**

```
*-------------------------------------------------------------*
| Create and sort data set MISSING as in PROBLEM 4.           |
*-------------------------------------------------------------*;
DATA FIRST;
   SET MISSING (KEEP=ID GENDER HEIGHT);
   BY ID;
   IF FIRST.ID;
RUN;

DATA BASKET;
   MERGE MISSING(DROP=GENDER HEIGHT) FIRST;
   BY ID;
RUN;

PROC PRINT DATA=BASKET;
   TITLE 'Listing of data set BASKET';
RUN;
```

**SOLUTION TO PROBLEM 6**

```
*-------------------------------------------------------------*
| Create and sort data set CLIN_X as in PROBLEM 1.            |
*-------------------------------------------------------------*;
```

```
DATA DIFFER;
   SET CLIN_X;
   BY ID;
   RETAIN OLD_HR OLD_SBP OLD_DBP;
   IF FIRST.ID THEN DO;
      OLD_HR = HR;
      OLD_SBP = SBP;
      OLD_DBP = DBP;
   END;
   IF LAST.ID AND NOT FIRST.ID THEN DO;
      DIFF_HR = HR - OLD_HR;
      DIFF_SBP = SBP - OLD_SBP;
      DIFF_DBP = DBP - OLD_DBP;
      OUTPUT;
   END;
KEEP ID DIFF_HR DIFF_SBP DIFF_DBP;
RUN;

PROC PRINT DATA=DIFFER;
   TITLE 'Listing of data set DIFFER';
RUN;

 /*-----------------------------------------------------------*
  | Alternative Solution:                                      |
  | Another solution is offered here where only the first and  |
  | last observation per patient (for those patients with two  |
  | or more visits) are selected and the DIF function is used  |
  | to compute a difference.                                   |
  |                                                            |
  | DATA DIFFER;                                               |
  |    SET CLIN_X;                                             |
  |    BY ID;                                                  |
  |    IF (FIRST.ID OR LAST.ID) AND NOT                        |
  |       (FIRST.ID AND LAST.ID);                              |
  |    DIFF_HR = DIF(HR);                                      |
  |    DIFF_SBP = DIF(SBP);                                    |
  |    DIFF_DBP = DIF(DBP);                                    |
  |    IF LAST.ID THEN OUTPUT;                                 |
  |    KEEP ID DIFF_HR DIFF_SBP DIFF_DBP;                      |
  | RUN;                                                       |
  *-----------------------------------------------------------*/
```

**SOLUTION TO PROBLEM 7**

```
DATA DRUG;
   INPUT ID DATE : MMDDYY8. RX1-RX3;
   FORMAT DATE MMDDYY8.;
DATALINES;
1 10/21/95 1 0 0
1 10/22/95 2 0 1
1 10/23/95 0 0 1
2 09/02/95 1 1 1
2 09/03/95 1 1 1
3 11/11/95 0 2 1
3 11/15/95 0 0 2
;
PROC SORT DATA=DRUG;
   BY ID DATE;
RUN;

DATA _NULL_;
   SET DRUG END=LAST;
   BY ID;
```

```
   FILE PRINT;
   ARRAY RX[3] RX1-RX3;
   ARRAY C[3] C1-C3;
   ARRAY RX_CNT[3] RX_CNT1-RX_CNT3;
   RETAIN C1-C3;

   ***Initialize flag for each subject;
   IF FIRST.ID THEN DO I = 1 TO 3;
      C[I] = 0;
   END;

   ***If a patient ever took a drug, C[I] is set to 1.
      It stays at 1 because of the RETAIN statement;
   DO I = 1 TO 3;
      IF RX[I] = 1 or RX[I] = 2 THEN C[I]=1;
   END;

   ***Accumulate a total for each of the 3 drugs;
   IF LAST.ID THEN DO I = 1 TO 3;
      RX_CNT[I] + C[I];
   END;

   ***Output if you reach the end of the file;
   IF LAST THEN PUT 'Number of people on drug 1 is ' RX_CNT1 /
                    'Number of people on drug 2 is ' RX_CNT2 /
                    'Number of people on drug 3 is ' RX_CNT3;

RUN;
```

# CHAPTER 11 Writing Simple DATA Step Reports

## SOLUTION TO PROBLEM 1

```
LIBNAME WORKBOOK 'C:\WORKBOOK';
OPTIONS FMTSEARCH=(WORKBOOK);

DATA _NULL_;
   TITLE 'Simple "No Frills" Report';
   SET WORKBOOK.CLINICAL(KEEP=ID SBP DBP);
   FILE PRINT;
   PUT ID SBP DBP;
RUN;
```

## SOLUTION TO PROBLEM 2

```
LIBNAME WORKBOOK 'C:\WORKBOOK';
OPTIONS FMTSEARCH=(WORKBOOK);

OPTIONS NODATE NONUMBER;

DATA _NULL_;
   TITLE;
   SET WORKBOOK.CLINICAL(KEEP=ID SBP DBP);
   FILE PRINT HEADER=CLIN_HDR;
   PUT  @4  ID  $3.
       @18 SBP  3.
       @38 DBP  3.;
   RETURN;
CLIN_HDR:
   PUT #1 @1 'Listing of Systolic and Diastolic Blood Pressure'
       #3 @5 'ID'  @15 'Systolic'  @35 'Diastolic'
       #4 @12 'Blood Pressure'  @32 'Blood Pressure'
       #5 @1 '------------------------------------------------';
RUN;
```

## SOLUTION TO PROBLEM 3

```
*------------------------------------*
| Solution using trailing at sign (@) |
*------------------------------------*;
LIBNAME WORKBOOK 'C:\WORKBOOK';
OPTIONS FMTSEARCH=(WORKBOOK);

OPTIONS NODATE NONUMBER;

DATA _NULL_;
   TITLE;
   SET WORKBOOK.CLINICAL(KEEP=ID SBP DBP);
   FILE PRINT HEADER=CLIN_HDR;
   PUT  @4 ID   $3.
       @18 SBP  3. @;
   IF SBP > 160 THEN PUT '*' @;
   PUT  @38 DBP  3. @;
   IF DBP > 90 THEN PUT '*';
      ELSE PUT;
   RETURN;
CLIN_HDR:
   PUT #1 @1 'Listing of Systolic and Diastolic Blood Pressure'
       #2 @1 ' (Pressures marked with an asterisk (*) are hypertensive)'
       #4 @5 'ID'  @15 'Systolic'  @35 'Diastolic'
       #5 @12 'Blood Pressure'  @32 'Blood Pressure'
       #6 @1 48*'-';
RUN;
```

```
*----------------------------------------------------*
| Solution using character variables and the SUBSTR  |
| pseudo function                                     |
*----------------------------------------------------*;
LIBNAME WORKBOOK 'C:\WORKBOOK';
OPTIONS FMTSEARCH=(WORKBOOK);
OPTIONS NODATE NONUMBER;

DATA _NULL_;
   TITLE;
   SET WORKBOOK.CLINICAL(KEEP=ID SBP DBP);
   FILE PRINT HEADER=CLIN_HDR;
   LENGTH C_SBP C_DBP $ 4;
   C_SBP = PUT(SBP,3.);
   C_DBP = PUT(DBP,3.);
   IF SBP > 160 THEN SUBSTR(C_SBP,4,1) = '*';
   IF DBP >  90 THEN SUBSTR(C_DBP,4,1) = '*';
   PUT  @4  ID    $3.
        @18 C_SBP $4.
        @38 C_DBP $4.;
   RETURN;
CLIN_HDR:
   PUT #1 @1 'Listing of Systolic and Diastolic Blood Pressure'
       #2 @1 ' (Pressures marked with an * are hypertensive)'
       #4 @5 'ID'  @15 'Systolic'  @35 'Diastolic'
       #5 @12 'Blood Pressure'  @32 'Blood Pressure'
       #6 @1 '--------------------------------------------------';
RUN;
```

## SOLUTION TO PROBLEM 4

```
LIBNAME WORKBOOK 'C:\WORKBOOK';
OPTIONS FMTSEARCH=(WORKBOOK);

OPTIONS LS=80 PS=25 NODATE NONUMBER;

DATA _NULL_;
   TITLE;
   FILE PRINT HEADER=CLIN_HDR N=PAGESIZE;
   DO COLUMN = 1,35;
      DO ROW = 6 TO 14;
         SET WORKBOOK.CLINICAL(KEEP=ID SBP DBP);
         PUT  #ROW @COLUMN+4   ID    $3.
                   @COLUMN+15  SBP    3.
                   @COLUMN+25  DBP    3.;
      END;
   END;
   PUT _PAGE_;
   RETURN;
CLIN_HDR:
   PUT #1 @10  'Listing of Systolic and Diastolic Blood Pressure'
       #3 @5   'ID'  @13 'Systolic'  @23 'Diastolic'
          @39  'ID'  @47 'Systolic'  @57 'Diastolic'
       #4 @17 'BP'  @27 'BP'  @51 'BP'  @61 'BP'
       #5 @1   68*'-';
RUN;
```

# CHAPTER 12 The FORMAT Procedure

## SOLUTION TO PROBLEM 1

```
PROC FORMAT;
   VALUE $GENDER 'M' = 'Male'
                 'F' = 'Female';
   VALUE AGEFMT   1 =  '0 TO 20'
                  2 = '21 TO 40'
                  3 = '41 TO 60'
                  4 = 'Greater than 60';
   VALUE $LIKERT  '1' = 'Strongly Disagree'
                  '2' = 'Disagree'
                  '3' = 'No Opinion'
                  '4' = 'Agree'
                  '5' = 'Strongly Agree';
RUN;

DATA SURVEY;
   INPUT @1 ID        $3.
         @4 GENDER    $1.
         @5 AGEGROUP  1.
         @6 (QUES1-QUES3)($1.);
   FORMAT GENDER $GENDER.
          AGEGROUP AGEFMT.
          QUES1-QUES3 $LIKERT.;
DATALINES;
001M1123
002F3452
003M2421
004F4531
;
PROC PRINT DATA=SURVEY NOOBS;
   TITLE 'Listing of Data Set SURVEY';
RUN;
```

## SOLUTION TO PROBLEM 2

```
PROC FORMAT;
   VALUE AGEGRP    LOW - <20 = 'Less than 20'
                   20 - <40  = '20 to less than 40'
                   40 - <60  = '40 to less than 60'
                   60 - HIGH = '60 and above';
   VALUE INS_CODE   1 = 'Not Insured'
                    2 = 'Gold Star Insurance'
                    3 = 'Blue Star Insurance'
                    4 = 'State Insurance'
                    5 = 'Medicare';
   VALUE $PAYCODE  '1','3','5' = 'Bill Paid'
                   '2'         = '30 Days Overdue'
                   'X','Y'     = 'Error in Billing'
                   '4'         = 'Collection Agency';
RUN;

DATA SURVEY_2;
   INPUT @1  ID   $3.
         @5  AGE   5.
         @10 CODE  1.
         @12 PAY  $1.;
FORMAT AGE     AGEGRP.
       CODE    INS_CODE.
       PAY     $PAYCODE.;
DATALINES;
001 23.0 1 1
```

```
002 55.9 2 3
003 60.1 3 2
004 12.5 1 5
005 19.1 5 X
;
PROC PRINT DATA=SURVEY_2 NOOBS;
   TITLE 'Listing of Data Set SURVEY_2';
RUN;
```

## SOLUTION TO PROBLEM 3

```
***Solution using the default libref LIBRARY;
LIBNAME LIBRARY 'C:\WORKBOOK';

PROC FORMAT LIBRARY=LIBRARY;
   VALUE $GENDER 'M' = 'Male'
                 'F' = 'Female';
   VALUE AGEFMT   1 =  '0 TO 20'
                  2 = '21 TO 40'
                  3 = '41 TO 60'
                  4 = 'Greater than 60';
RUN;

***At a later session;
LIBNAME LIBRARY 'C:\WORKBOOK';

DATA SURVEY;
   INPUT @1 ID        $3.
         @4 GENDER    $1.
         @5 AGEGROUP   1.
         @6 (QUES1-QUES3)($1.);
   FORMAT GENDER $GENDER.
          AGEGROUP AGEFMT.
          QUES1-QUES3 $LIKERT.;
DATALINES;
001M1123
002F3452
003M2421
004F4531
;
PROC PRINT DATA=SURVEY NOOBS;
   TITLE 'Listing of Data Set SURVEY';
RUN;

***Solution using another LIBNAME;
LIBNAME MYFORMAT 'C:\WORKBOOK';

PROC FORMAT LIBRARY=MYFORMAT;
   VALUE $GENDER 'M' = 'Male'
                 'F' = 'Female';
   VALUE AGEFMT   1 =  '0 TO 20'
                  2 = '21 TO 40'
                  3 = '41 TO 60'
                  4 = 'Greater than 60';
RUN;

***At a later session;
LIBNAME MYFORMAT 'C:\WORKBOOK';
OPTIONS FMTSEARCH=(MYFORMAT);

DATA SURVEY;
   INPUT @1 ID        $3.
         @4 GENDER    $1.
```

```
         @5 AGEGROUP  1.
         @6 (QUES1-QUES3)($1.);
   FORMAT GENDER $GENDER.
          AGEGROUP AGEFMT.
          QUES1-QUES3 $LIKERT.;
DATALINES;
00111123
00223452
00312421
00424531
;
PROC PRINT DATA=SURVEY NOOBS;
   TITLE 'Listing of Data Set SURVEY';
RUN;
```

## SOLUTION TO PROBLEM 4

```
DATA CODES;
   INPUT @1  DX_CODE $2.
         @4  DESCRIP $16.;
DATALINES;
01 Cold
02 Flu
03 Break or Fracture
04 Routine Physical
05 Heart Problem
06 Lung Disorder
07 Abdominal Pain
08 Laceration
09 Immunization
10 Lyme Disease
11 Ear Ache
;
DATA FRODO;
   SET CODES (RENAME=(DX_CODE=START
                      DESCRIP=LABEL));
   RETAIN FMTNAME '$DXFMT'
          TYPE    'C';
RUN;

PROC FORMAT CNTLIN=FRODO FMTLIB;
RUN;
```

## SOLUTION TO PROBLEM 5

```
DATA ZIP;
   INPUT ZIP_CODE LOCATION & $20.;
DATALINES;
08822 Flemington, NJ
11518 East Rockaway, NY
08903 New Brunswick, NJ
;
DATA BILBO;
   SET ZIP (RENAME=(ZIP_CODE=START
                    LOCATION=LABEL));
   RETAIN FMTNAME 'ZIPFMT'
          TYPE    'N';
RUN;

PROC FORMAT CNTLIN=BILBO FMTLIB;
RUN;
```

## SOLUTION TO PROBLEM 6

```
PROC FORMAT;
   INVALUE LEAD LOW-HIGH = _SAME_
                'A'      = .1
                'B'      = .05
                'C'      = .5
                OTHER    = .;
RUN;

DATA LEAD;
   INPUT LEVEL : LEAD. @@;
DATALINES;
5.6 A 2.0 2.1 C 9 B 3.7 X 10
;
PROC PRINT DATA=LEAD;
   TITLE 'Listing of Data Set LEAD';
RUN;
```

## SOLUTION TO PROBLEM 7

```
DATA MISSING;
   INFILE DATALINES PAD;
   INPUT @1  GROUP  $1.
         @3  GENDER $1.
         @5  (X Y Z)(1.+1);
DATALINES;
A M 1 2 3

B F 1   6
A     9 3
M   5 6 7
a f 5 6 7
* $ 9 9 9
;
PROC FORMAT;
   VALUE XMISS LOW-HIGH = 'NON-MISSING'
               . = 'MISSING';
   VALUE $CMISS 'a' - 'z',
                'A' - 'Z',
                '*','$' = 'NON-MISSING'
                OTHER = 'MISSING';
RUN;

PROC FREQ DATA=MISSING;
   TABLES _ALL_ / NOCUM MISSING;
   FORMAT _NUMERIC_ XMISS.
          _CHARACTER_ $CMISS.;
RUN;
```

# CHAPTER 13 The PRINT Procedure

### SOLUTION TO PROBLEM 1

```
LIBNAME WORKBOOK 'C:\WORKBOOK';
OPTIONS FMTSEARCH=(WORKBOOK);

PROC PRINT DATA=WORKBOOK.CLINICAL(OBS=10);
   ID ID;
   VAR DOB VISIT PRIM_DX;
RUN;
```

### SOLUTION TO PROBLEM 2

```
LIBNAME WORKBOOK 'C:\WORKBOOK';
OPTIONS FMTSEARCH=(WORKBOOK);

PROC PRINT DATA=WORKBOOK.CLINICAL(OBS=10) NOOBS LABEL;
   VAR ID DOB VISIT PRIM_DX;
   LABEL ID      = 'Patient ID'
         DOB     = 'Date of Birth'
         VISIT   = 'Date of Visit'
         PRIM_DX = 'Primary DX';
   FORMAT DOB VISIT DATE7.;
RUN;
```

### SOLUTION TO PROBLEM 3

```
LIBNAME WORKBOOK 'C:\WORKBOOK';
OPTIONS FMTSEARCH=(WORKBOOK);

PROC PRINT DATA=WORKBOOK.CLINICAL(OBS=10);
   TITLE1 'Sample Report from the Indian Point Clinic';
   TITLE2 '(Sample listing of the first ten cases)';
   TITLE3 '-----------------------------------------';
   FOOTNOTE '*** Prepared by Data Systems of Greater Flemington ***';
   ID ID;
   VAR DOB VISIT PRIM_DX;
RUN;
```

### SOLUTION TO PROBLEM 4

```
DATA BASKET;
   INFILE 'C:\WORKBOOK\BASKET.DTA' PAD;
   INPUT @1  ID     $3.
         @5  GENDER $1.
         @7  HEIGHT  2.
         @10 DATE    MMDDYY8.
         @19 POINTS  2.;
   FORMAT DATE MMDDYY8.;
RUN;

PROC SORT DATA=BASKET;
   BY GENDER;
RUN;

PROC PRINT DATA=BASKET NOOBS;
   BY GENDER;
   TITLE 'Listing of Basketball Statistics - Grouped by Gender';
   VAR ID HEIGHT DATE POINTS;
RUN;
```

### SOLUTION TO PROBLEM 5

```
DATA BASKET;
   INFILE 'C:\WORKBOOK\BASKET.DTA' PAD;
   INPUT @1  ID $3.
```

```
           @5  GENDER $1.
           @7  HEIGHT  2.
           @10 DATE    MMDDYY8.
           @19 POINTS  2.;
   FORMAT DATE MMDDYY8.;
RUN;

PROC SORT DATA=BASKET;
   BY GENDER;
RUN;

PROC FORMAT;
   VALUE $GENDER 'M' = 'Male'
                 'F' = 'Female';
RUN;

OPTIONS NOBYLINE;

PROC PRINT DATA=BASKET NOOBS;
   BY GENDER;
   FORMAT GENDER $GENDER.;
   TITLE 'Report on the #BYVAL(GENDER) Basketball Players';
   VAR ID HEIGHT DATE POINTS;
RUN;
```

## SOLUTION TO PROBLEM 6

```
DATA BASKET;
   INFILE 'C:\WORKBOOK\BASKET.DTA' PAD;
   INPUT @1  ID      $3.
         @5  GENDER $1.
         @7  HEIGHT  2.
         @10 DATE    MMDDYY8.
         @19 POINTS  2.;
RUN;

PROC SORT DATA=BASKET;
   BY GENDER ID;
RUN;

PROC FORMAT;
   VALUE $GENDER 'M' = 'Male'
                 'F' = 'Female';
RUN;

OPTIONS NOBYLINE NODATE NONUMBER CENTER LS=64 PS=54;

PROC PRINT DATA=BASKET NOOBS LABEL N;
   BY GENDER;
   LABEL ID     = 'Employee Number'
         POINTS = 'Points per Game'
         DATE   = 'Date';
   FORMAT GENDER $GENDER. DATE WORDDATE.;
   TITLE1 'The ABC Company Basketball Team Roster';
   TITLE2 'Data for the #BYVAL(GENDER) Players';
   TITLE3 '-------------------------------------';
   ID ID;
   VAR DATE POINTS;
   SUM POINTS;
RUN;
```

# CHAPTER 14 The SORT Procedure

## SOLUTION TO PROBLEM 1

```
DATA CARS;
   INFILE 'C:\WORKBOOK\CARS.DTA' PAD;
   INPUT  @ 1 SIZE     $9.
          @11 MANUFACT $9.
          @22 MODEL    $9.
          @38 MILEAGE   2.
          @50 RELIABLE  1.;
RUN;

***Part A;
PROC SORT DATA=CARS;
   BY RELIABLE;
RUN;

PROC PRINT DATA=CARS;
   TITLE 'Listing from Default Sort';
RUN;

***Part B;
PROC SORT DATA=CARS;
   BY DESCENDING RELIABLE;
RUN;

PROC PRINT DATA=CARS;
   TITLE 'Listing from Descending Sort';
RUN;

***Part C;
PROC SORT DATA=CARS;
   BY MANUFACT DESCENDING SIZE;
RUN;

PROC PRINT DATA=CARS NOOBS;
   TITLE 'Listing Sorted by Manufacturer and Size';
   VAR MANUFACT SIZE;
RUN;
```

## SOLUTION TO PROBLEM 2

```
LIBNAME WORKBOOK 'C:\WORKBOOK';
OPTIONS FMTSEARCH=(WORKBOOK);

***Part A;

*--------------------------------------------------------*
| Notice the use of a LABEL= data set option on the output|
| data set.  This was requested as an optional task       |
| in the problem.  Data set labels are very useful since  |
| they remain with the data sets and show up when you run |
| PROC CONTENTS.                                          |
*--------------------------------------------------------*;
PROC SORT DATA=WORKBOOK.CLINICAL
          OUT=SORTED(LABEL='Clinical data in ID Order');
   BY ID;
RUN;

PROC PRINT DATA=SORTED;
   TITLE 'Data Set SORTED Created from CLINICAL';
RUN;
```

```
***Part B;
PROC SORT DATA=WORKBOOK.CLINICAL(WHERE=(SBP > 160))
          OUT=SUBSET1(LABEL='Clinical Data SBP > 160');
   BY ID;
RUN;

PROC PRINT DATA=SUBSET1;
   TITLE 'Data Set SUBSET1 Created from CLINICAL';
RUN;

***Part C;
PROC SORT DATA=WORKBOOK.CLINICAL(KEEP=ID SBP DBP)
          OUT=SUBSET2(LABEL='Clinical Data ID, SBP,and DBP');
   BY ID;
RUN;

PROC PRINT DATA=SUBSET2;
   TITLE 'Data Set SUBSET2 Created from CLINICAL';
RUN;



***Part D;
PROC SORT DATA=WORKBOOK.CLINICAL(KEEP=ID SBP DBP
                                 WHERE=(SBP > 160))
          OUT=SUBSET3(LABEL='Clinical data: SBP > 160, ID, and DBP');
   BY ID;
RUN;

PROC PRINT DATA=SUBSET3;
   TITLE 'Data Set SUBSET3 Created from CLINICAL';
RUN;
```

### SOLUTION TO PROBLEM 3

```
DATA DUP1;
   INPUT NAME $ X Y;
DATALINES;
ADAM    2 3
ADAM    2 3
CHARLES 4 7
ADAM    4 5
DAVID   8 9
CHARLES 9 9
;
PROC PRINT DATA=DUP1;
   TITLE 'Listing of Data Set DUP1 before the sort';
RUN;

***Part A;
PROC SORT DATA=DUP1 OUT=TMP NODUPKEY;
   BY NAME;
RUN;

PROC PRINT DATA=TMP;
   TITLE 'Listing with Option NODUPKEY Used';
RUN;

***Part B;
PROC SORT DATA=DUP1 OUT=TMP NODUP;
   BY NAME;
RUN;
```

```
PROC PRINT DATA=TMP;
   TITLE 'Listing with Option NODUP Used';
RUN;

***Part C;
DATA DUP2;
   INPUT NAME $ X Y;
DATALINES;
ADAM    2 3
CHARLES 4 7
ADAM    4 5
ADAM    2 3
DAVID   8 9
CHARLES 9 9
;
PROC SORT DATA=DUP2 OUT=TMP NODUP;
   BY NAME;
RUN;

PROC PRINT DATA=TMP;
   TITLE 'Listing with Option NODUP Used (alternate ordering)';
RUN;

***Part D;

*---------------------------------------------------------*
| By using all three variables, NAME, X, and Y, as BY     |
| variables, the NODUPKEY or NODUP option will remove the |
| observations that were not adjacent but were duplicates |
*---------------------------------------------------------*;
PROC SORT DATA=DUP2 OUT=TMP NODUPKEY;
   BY NAME X Y;
RUN;

PROC PRINT DATA=TMP;
   TITLE 'Listing with Option NODUPKEY and multiple BY variables';
RUN;
```

### SOLUTION TO PROBLEM 4

```
DATA TEST_EQ;
   INPUT A B @@;
DATALINES;
1 8 1 5 2 5 1 7
;
PROC SORT DATA=TEST_EQ OUT=TMP;
   BY A;
RUN;

PROC PRINT DATA=TMP;
   TITLE 'Data Set Without the NOEQUALS Option';
RUN;

PROC SORT DATA=TEST_EQ NOEQUALS OUT=TMP;
   BY A;
RUN;

*---------------------------------------------------------*
| The NOEQUALS option does not necessarily maintain the   |
| original order of the observations for identical values |
| of the BY variable(s).                                  |
*---------------------------------------------------------*;
```

```
PROC PRINT DATA=TMP;
   TITLE 'Data Set With the NOEQUALS Option';
RUN;
```

# CHAPTER 15 The FREQ Procedure

### SOLUTION TO PROBLEM 1

```
DATA CARS;
   INFILE 'C:\WORKBOOK\CARS.DTA' PAD;
   INPUT  @ 1 SIZE     $9.
          @11 MANUFACT $9.
          @22 MODEL    $9.
          @38 MILEAGE   2.
          @50 RELIABLE  1.;
RUN;

PROC FREQ DATA=CARS;
   TITLE 'Frequencies from CARS Data Set';
   TABLES SIZE MANUFACT;
RUN;
```

### SOLUTION TO PROBLEM 2

```
*-------------------------------------------------------------*
| Data set CARS created in PROBLEM 1                          |
*-------------------------------------------------------------*;
PROC FREQ DATA=CARS;
   TITLE 'Frequencies using options NOPERCENT and NOCOM';
   TABLES SIZE MANUFACT / NOPERCENT NOCUM;
RUN;
```

### SOLUTION TO PROBLEM 3

```
LIBNAME WORKBOOK 'C:\WORKBOOK';
OPTIONS FMTSEARCH=(WORKBOOK);

PROC FREQ DATA=WORKBOOK.CLINICAL;
   TITLE 'Frequencies from CLINICAL without the MISSING Option';
   TABLES SEC_DX;
RUN;

PROC FREQ DATA=WORKBOOK.CLINICAL;
   TITLE 'Frequencies from CLINICAL with the MISSING Option';
   TABLES SEC_DX / MISSING;
RUN;
```

### SOLUTION TO PROBLEM 4

```
LIBNAME WORKBOOK 'C:\WORKBOOK';
OPTIONS FMTSEARCH=(WORKBOOK);

PROC FREQ DATA=WORKBOOK.CLINICAL ORDER=DATA;
   TITLE 'Frequencies from CLINICAL with ORDER=DATA';
   TABLES PRIM_DX;
RUN;

PROC FREQ DATA=WORKBOOK.CLINICAL ORDER=FORMATTED;
   TITLE 'Frequencies from CLINICAL with ORDER=FORMATTED';
   TABLES PRIM_DX;
RUN;

PROC FREQ DATA=WORKBOOK.CLINICAL ORDER=FREQ;
   TITLE 'Frequencies from CLINICAL with ORDER=FREQ';
   TABLES PRIM_DX;
RUN;
```

```
PROC FREQ DATA=WORKBOOK.CLINICAL ORDER=INTERNAL;
   TITLE 'Frequencies from CLINICAL with ORDER=INTERNAL';
   TABLES PRIM_DX;
RUN;
```

### SOLUTION TO PROBLEM 5

```
DATA DEMOG1;
   INFILE 'C:\WORKBOOK\DEMOG1.DTA' PAD;
   INPUT  @1  ID       $3.
          @4  DOB       MMDDYY6.
          @10 GENDER   $1.
          @11 STATE    $2.
          @13 EMPLOYED $1.;
   FORMAT DOB MMDDYY8.;
RUN;

PROC FREQ DATA=DEMOG1;
   TITLE 'Frequencies from DEMOG1';
   TABLES GENDER*EMPLOYED;
RUN;

PROC FREQ DATA=DEMOG1;
   TITLE 'Frequencies from DEMOG1 - LIST Option';
   TABLES GENDER*EMPLOYED / LIST;
RUN;
```

### SOLUTION TO PROBLEM 6

```
PROC FORMAT;
   VALUE YESNO 1='YES' 0='NO';
RUN;

DATA CPR;
   INFILE 'C:\WORKBOOK\CPR.DTA';
   INPUT SUBJECT  1-3
         V_FIB     4
         RESP      5
         AGEGROUP  6
         SURVIVE   7;

   LABEL V_FIB = 'PT IN V-FIB?'
         RESP   = 'PT ON RESPIRATOR?'
         AGEGROUP = 'AGE >= 70?'
         SURVIVE  = 'DID PT SURVIVE?';

   FORMAT V_FIB RESP SURVIVE YESNO.;
RUN;

PROC FREQ DATA=CPR;
   TITLE 'Frequencies from CPR';
   TABLES (V_FIB RESP AGEGROUP)*SURVIVE;
RUN;
```

### SOLUTION TO PROBLEM 7

```
LIBNAME WORKBOOK 'C:\WORKBOOK';
OPTIONS FMTSEARCH=(WORKBOOK);

PROC FREQ DATA=WORKBOOK.CLINICAL;
   TABLES PRIM_DX SEC_DX / NOPRINT
                           OUT=COUNTS (DROP=PERCENT);
RUN;
```

```
PROC PRINT DATA=COUNTS;
   TITLE 'Listing of Data Set COUNTS';
RUN;
```

### SOLUTION TO PROBLEM 8

```
*-------------------------------------------------------*
| Data set DEMOG1 created in Problem 5                  |
*-------------------------------------------------------*;
PROC FREQ DATA=DEMOG1;
   TITLE 'Three-way Table';
   TABLES STATE*GENDER*EMPLOYED;
RUN;
```

### SOLUTION TO PROBLEM 9

```
PROC FORMAT;
   VALUE MILE 0-9       = '0 TO 9'
              10-19     = '10 TO 19'
              20-29     = '20 TO 29'
              30 - HIGH = '30 AND ABOVE';
RUN;

*-------------------------------------------------------*
| Data set CARS created in Problem 1                    |
*-------------------------------------------------------*;
PROC FREQ DATA=CARS;
   TITLE 'Frequencies Grouped by a Format';
   TABLES MILEAGE*SIZE;
   FORMAT MILEAGE MILE.;
RUN;
```

### SOLUTION TO PROBLEM 10

```
LIBNAME WORKBOOK 'C:\WORKBOOK';
OPTIONS FMTSEARCH=(WORKBOOK);

*-------------------------------------------------------*
| This solution displays MONTH as a number from 1 to 12. |
*-------------------------------------------------------*;
PROC FREQ DATA=WORKBOOK.CLINICAL;
   TITLE 'Frequencies Grouped by Built-In Formats';
   TABLES VISIT;
   FORMAT VISIT MONTH.;
RUN;

*------------------------------------------------------------*
| This solution displays MONTH as a three-letter abbreviation. |
*------------------------------------------------------------*;
PROC FREQ DATA=WORKBOOK.CLINICAL;
   TITLE 'Frequencies Grouped by Built-In Formats';
   TABLES VISIT;
   FORMAT VISIT MONNAME3.;
RUN;

*------------------------------------------------------------*
| This solution displays day of the week as a three-letter    |
| character abbreviation.  The list is NOT in day order.      |
*------------------------------------------------------------*;
PROC FREQ DATA=WORKBOOK.CLINICAL;
   TITLE 'Frequencies Grouped by Built-In Formats';
   TABLES VISIT;
   FORMAT VISIT DOWNAME3.;  ***Or WEEKDATE3.;
RUN;
```

```
*-------------------------------------------------------------*
| Solution to list the days of the week in day order.         |
*-------------------------------------------------------------*;
DATA TMP;
   SET WORKBOOK.CLINICAL (KEEP=VISIT);
   DAY = WEEKDAY(VISIT);
RUN;

PROC SORT DATA=TMP;
   BY DAY;
RUN;

PROC FREQ DATA=TMP ORDER=DATA; ***The key is the ORDER= option;
   TITLE 'Frequencies Grouped by Day of the Week in Proper Order';
   TABLES VISIT;
   FORMAT VISIT DOWNAME3.;
RUN;
```

# CHAPTER 16 The MEANS Procedure

## SOLUTION TO PROBLEM 1

```
*------------------------------------------------------------*
| For this solution, the CARS data set is created with all the |
| variables so that it can be used in the other problems in    |
| this chapter.                                                |
*------------------------------------------------------------*;
DATA CARS;
   INFILE 'C:\WORKBOOK\CARS.DTA' PAD;

   INPUT @1  SIZE      $9.
         @11 MANUFACT  $9.
         @22 MODEL     $9.
         @38 MILEAGE    2.
         @50 RELIABLE   1.;
RUN;

PROC MEANS DATA=CARS N NMISS MEAN MAXDEC=1;
   TITLE 'Output from Problem 1';
   VAR MILEAGE RELIABLE;
RUN;
```

## SOLUTION TO PROBLEM 2

```
*-------------------------------------------------------*
| Data set CARS created in PROBLEM 1                     |
*-------------------------------------------------------*;
PROC MEANS DATA=CARS N NMISS MEAN MAXDEC=1;
   CLASS SIZE;
   TITLE 'Output from Problem 2';
   VAR MILEAGE RELIABLE;
RUN;
```

## SOLUTION TO PROBLEM 3

```
*-------------------------------------------------------*
| Data set CARS created in PROBLEM 1                     |
*-------------------------------------------------------*;
PROC MEANS DATA=CARS NOPRINT NWAY;
   CLASS SIZE;
   VAR MILEAGE RELIABLE;
   OUTPUT OUT =CAR_AVE(DROP=_TYPE_ _FREQ_)
          MEAN=M_RELIAB M_MILE
          N   =N_RELIAB N_MILE;
RUN;

PROC PRINT DATA=CAR_AVE NOOBS;
   TITLE 'Output from Problem 3';
RUN;
```

## SOLUTION TO PROBLEM 4

```
*-------------------------------------------------------*
| Data set CARS created in PROBLEM 1                     |
*-------------------------------------------------------*;
PROC MEANS DATA=CARS NOPRINT NWAY;
   CLASS MANUFACT SIZE;
   VAR MILEAGE RELIABLE;
   OUTPUT OUT =CAR_MEAN(DROP=_TYPE_ _FREQ_)
          MEAN=M_RELIAB M_MILE
          N   =N_RELIAB N_MILE;
RUN;
```

```
PROC PRINT DATA=CAR_MEAN NOOBS;
   TITLE 'Output from Problem 4';
RUN;
```

**SOLUTION TO PROBLEM 5**

```
DATA MISSING;
   INFILE DATALINES PAD;
   INPUT GROUP $ 1 GENDER $ 3 @5 (X Y Z)(1.+1);
DATALINES;
A M 1 2 3

B F 1   6
A     9 3
  M 5 6 7
a f 5 6 7
* $ 9 9 9
;
PROC MEANS NOPRINT DATA=MISSING;
   VAR _NUMERIC_;
   OUTPUT OUT=MISS_CNT (RENAME=(_FREQ_ = TOTAL) DROP=_TYPE_)
                      N=NX NY NZ
                      NMISS = NMX NMY NMZ;
RUN;

PROC PRINT DATA=MISS_CNT LABEL NOOBS;
   TITLE 'Number of Missing and Non-missing Values';
   LABEL NX     = 'X Non-missing'
         NY     = 'Y Non-missing'
         NZ     = 'Z Non-missing'
         NMX    = 'X Missing'
         NMY    = 'Y Missing'
         NMZ    = 'Z Missing'
         TOTAL   = 'Total';
   VAR TOTAL NX NMX NY NMX NZ NMZ;
RUN;
```

# CHAPTER 17 The TABULATE Procedure

## SOLUTION TO PROBLEM 1

```
LIBNAME WORKBOOK 'C:\WORKBOOK';
OPTIONS CENTER FMTSEARCH=(WORKBOOK) NODATE NONUMBER;

PROC TABULATE DATA=WORKBOOK.CLINICAL;
   TITLE 'Simple One-way Table';
   CLASS GENDER;
   TABLE GENDER;
RUN;
```

## SOLUTION TO PROBLEM 2

```
LIBNAME WORKBOOK 'C:\WORKBOOK';
OPTIONS CENTER FMTSEARCH=(WORKBOOK) NODATE NONUMBER;

PROC TABULATE DATA=WORKBOOK.CLINICAL;
   TITLE 'Two-way Table';
   CLASS GENDER VITAMINS;
   TABLE GENDER ALL,VITAMINS ALL;
RUN;
```

## SOLUTION TO PROBLEM 3

```
LIBNAME WORKBOOK 'C:\WORKBOOK';
OPTIONS CENTER FMTSEARCH=(WORKBOOK) NODATE NONUMBER;

PROC TABULATE DATA=WORKBOOK.CLINICAL FORMAT=7.;
   TITLE 'Counts and Percentages in a Two-way Table';
   CLASS GENDER VITAMINS;

   TABLE  GENDER ALL,
          (VITAMINS ALL)*(N PCTN) / RTSPACE=25;

   KEYLABEL ALL     = 'All'
            N       = 'Number'
            PCTN    = 'Percent';

   LABEL    GENDER   = 'Patient Gender'
            VITAMINS = 'Taking Vitamins?';

RUN;
```

## SOLUTION TO PROBLEM 4

```
LIBNAME WORKBOOK 'C:\WORKBOOK';
OPTIONS CENTER FMTSEARCH=(WORKBOOK) NODATE NONUMBER;

PROC TABULATE DATA=WORKBOOK.CLINICAL FORMAT=7.0;
   TITLE 'Selecting a Denominator for a Percentage';
   CLASS GENDER VITAMINS;

   TABLE  GENDER ALL,
          VITAMINS*(N PCTN<VITAMINS>) ALL / RTS=20;

   KEYLABEL ALL     = 'All'
            N       = 'Number'
            PCTN    = 'Percent';

   LABEL    GENDER   = 'Gender'
            VITAMINS = 'Taking Vitamins?';

RUN;
```

## SOLUTION TO PROBLEM 5

```
LIBNAME WORKBOOK 'C:\WORKBOOK';
OPTIONS CENTER FMTSEARCH=(WORKBOOK) NODATE NONUMBER;

*-------------------------------------------------------------*
| Need to create a new data set with month and day of visit   |
*-------------------------------------------------------------*;
DATA NEW;
   SET WORKBOOK.CLINICAL;
   MONTH = MONTH(VISIT);
   DAY = WEEKDAY(VISIT);
RUN;


*-------------------------------------------------------------*
| Formats for MONTH and DAY                                   |
*-------------------------------------------------------------*;
PROC FORMAT;
   VALUE MONFMT 1='Jan' 2='Feb' 3='Mar' 4='Apr' 5='May' 6='Jun'
                7='Jul' 8='Aug' 9='Sep' 10='Oct' 11='Nov' 12='Dec';
   VALUE DAYFMT 1='Sun' 2='Mon' 3='Tue' 4='Wed' 5='Thu' 6='Fri' 7='Sat';
RUN;

PROC TABULATE DATA=NEW FORMAT=5. ;
   TITLE 'Three-way Table - Visits by Gender, Month, and Day of Visit';
   CLASS GENDER MONTH DAY;
   TABLE GENDER, MONTH, DAY / PRINTMISS BOX=_PAGE_ MISSTEXT=' ';

   LABEL GENDER = 'Gender'
         MONTH  = 'Month of Visit'
         DAY    = 'Day of Visit';

   KEYLABEL N    = 'Count';

   FORMAT MONTH MONFMT. DAY DAYFMT.;
RUN;
```

## SOLUTION TO PROBLEM 6

```
LIBNAME WORKBOOK 'C:\WORKBOOK';
OPTIONS CENTER FMTSEARCH=(WORKBOOK) NODATE NONUMBER;

*-------------------------------------------------------------*
| Need to create a new data set with month and day of visit   |
*-------------------------------------------------------------*;
DATA NEW;
   SET WORKBOOK.CLINICAL;
   MONTH = MONTH(VISIT);
   DAY = WEEKDAY(VISIT);
RUN;

*-------------------------------------------------------------*
| Formats for MONTH and DAY                                   |
*-------------------------------------------------------------*;
PROC FORMAT;
   VALUE MONFMT 1='Jan' 2='Feb' 3='Mar' 4='Apr' 5='May' 6='Jun'
                7='Jul' 8='Aug' 9='Sep' 10='Oct' 11='Nov' 12='Dec';
   VALUE DAYFMT 1='Sun' 2='Mon' 3='Tue' 4='Wed' 5='Thu' 6='Fri' 7='Sat';
RUN;

PROC TABULATE DATA=NEW FORMAT=3. ;
   TITLE1 'Three-way Table - Visits by Gender, Month, and Day of Visit';
```

```
   TITLE2 'Percentages Added';
   CLASS GENDER MONTH DAY;

   TABLE GENDER, MONTH, DAY*(N PCTN<DAY>) /
      PRINTMISS BOX=_PAGE_ MISSTEXT=' ';

   LABEL GENDER = 'Gender'
         MONTH  = 'Month of Visit'
         DAY    = 'Day of Visit';

   KEYLABEL N    = 'N'
            PCTN = '%';

   FORMAT MONTH MONFMT. DAY DAYFMT.;
RUN;
```

## SOLUTION TO PROBLEM 7

```
LIBNAME WORKBOOK 'C:\WORKBOOK';
OPTIONS CENTER FMTSEARCH=(WORKBOOK) NODATE NONUMBER;

PROC TABULATE DATA=WORKBOOK.CLINICAL FORMAT=8.0;
   TITLE 'Basic Descriptive Statistics';
   VAR HR DBP SBP;

   TABLE  HR SBP DBP,
          (N*F=7.0  NMISS MEAN*F=6.1 STD*F=6.2 MIN MAX) /
          RTSPACE=20;

   KEYLABEL N     = 'Number'
            NMISS = 'Missing'
            MEAN  = 'Mean'
            STD   = 'S.D.'
            MIN   = 'Minimum'
            MAX   = 'Maximum';

   LABEL HR  = 'Heart Rate'
         SBP = 'Systolic BP'
         DBP = 'Diastolic BP';

RUN;
```

## SOLUTION TO PROBLEM 8

```
LIBNAME WORKBOOK 'C:\WORKBOOK';
OPTIONS CENTER FMTSEARCH=(WORKBOOK) NODATE NONUMBER;

PROC TABULATE DATA=WORKBOOK.CLINICAL;
   TITLE 'Simple Statistics Broken Down by a Single Variable';
   CLASS GENDER;
   VAR HR DBP SBP;

   TABLE  (HR SBP DBP)*(N MEAN STD STDERR),
          (GENDER ALL) / RTS=30;

   KEYLABEL N      = 'Number'
            MEAN   = 'Mean'
            STD    = 'S.D.'
            STDERR = 'S.E.'
            ALL    = 'All';

   LABEL HR     = 'Heart Rate'
         SBP    = 'Systolic BP'
```

```
         DBP    = 'Diastolic BP'
         GENDER = 'Gender';
RUN;
```

## SOLUTION TO PROBLEM 9

```
LIBNAME WORKBOOK 'C:\WORKBOOK';
OPTIONS CENTER FMTSEARCH=(WORKBOOK) NODATE NONUMBER;

PROC TABULATE DATA=WORKBOOK.CLINICAL;
   TITLE 'Simple Statistics Broken Down by a Single Variable';
   CLASS GENDER;
   VAR HR DBP SBP;

   TABLE  (HR SBP DBP),
          (GENDER ALL)*(N*F=6.0  MEAN*F=5.1 STD*F=5.2) /
          RTSPACE=15;

   KEYLABEL N     = 'Number'
            MEAN  = 'Mean'
            STD   = 'S.D.';

LABEL HR     = 'Heart Rate'
      SBP    = 'Systolic BP'
      DBP    = 'Diastolic BP'
      GENDER = 'Gender';
RUN;
```

## SOLUTION TO PROBLEM 10

```
LIBNAME WORKBOOK 'C:\WORKBOOK';
OPTIONS CENTER FMTSEARCH=(WORKBOOK) NODATE NONUMBER;

PROC TABULATE DATA=WORKBOOK.CLINICAL FORMAT=8.0;
   TITLE1 'Basic Descriptive Statistics';
   TITLE2 'Broken Down by Gender';
   CLASS GENDER;
   VAR HR DBP SBP;

   TABLE  (HR SBP DBP)*(GENDER ALL),
          (N*F=7.0  NMISS MEAN*F=6.1 STD*F=6.2 MIN MAX) /
          RTSPACE=28 PRINTMISS BOX='Place Your Ad Here';

   KEYLABEL N     = 'Number'
            NMISS = 'Missing'
            MEAN  = 'Mean'
            STD   = 'S.D.'
            MIN   = 'Minimum'
            MAX   = 'Maximum'
            ALL   = 'Total';

   LABEL HR       = 'Heart Rate'
         SBP      = 'Systolic BP'
         DBP      = 'Diastolic BP'
         GENDER   = 'Gender';
RUN;
```

## SOLUTION TO PROBLEM 11

```
LIBNAME WORKBOOK 'C:\WORKBOOK';
OPTIONS CENTER FMTSEARCH=(WORKBOOK) NODATE NONUMBER;
```

```
PROC TABULATE DATA=WORKBOOK.CLINICAL;
   TITLE 'Simple Statistics Broken Down by Two Variables';
   CLASS GENDER VITAMINS;
   VAR HR DBP SBP;

   TABLE  (VITAMINS ALL)*(GENDER ALL),
          (HR SBP DBP)*(N*F=6.0  MEAN*F=5.1) /
          RTSPACE=37 PRINTMISS;

   KEYLABEL N      = 'Number'
            MEAN   = 'Mean'
            ALL    = 'Both';

   LABEL HR       = 'Heart Rate'
         SBP      = 'Systolic BP'
         DBP      = 'Diastolic BP'
         GENDER   = 'Gender'
         VITAMINS = 'Taking Vitamins?' ;
RUN;
```

# CHAPTER 18 The CHART Procedure

## SOLUTION TO PROBLEM 1

```
OPTIONS PS=48 LS=78; ***Pagesize chosen to make shorter charts;

*-------------------------------------------------------------*
| For this solution, the CARS data set is created with all the |
| variables so that it can be used in the other problems in    |
| this chapter.                                                |
*-------------------------------------------------------------*;
DATA CARS;
   INFILE 'C:\WORKBOOK\CARS.DTA' PAD;

   INPUT @1  SIZE      $9.
         @11 MANUFACT  $9.
         @22 MODEL     $9.
         @38 MILEAGE    2.
         @50 RELIABLE   1.;
RUN;

PROC CHART DATA=CARS;
   TITLE 'Simple Vertical Bar Chart';
   VBAR SIZE MANUFACT;
RUN;
```

## SOLUTION TO PROBLEM 2

```
*-------------------------------------------------------------*
| Data set CARS created in PROBLEM 1                           |
*-------------------------------------------------------------*;
PROC CHART DATA=CARS;
   TITLE 'Simple Horizontal Bar Chart';
   HBAR SIZE MANUFACT;
   HBAR SIZE MANUFACT / NOSTAT;
RUN;
```

## SOLUTION TO PROBLEM 3

```
*-------------------------------------------------------------*
| Data set CARS created in PROBLEM 1                           |
*-------------------------------------------------------------*;
PROC CHART DATA=CARS;
   TITLE 'Vertical Bar Chart Showing Percentages';
   VBAR SIZE / TYPE=PERCENT;
RUN;
```

## SOLUTION TO PROBLEM 4

```
*-------------------------------------------------------------*
| Data set CARS created in PROBLEM 1                           |
*-------------------------------------------------------------*;
PROC CHART DATA=CARS;
   TITLE1 'Vertical Bar Chart for a Numerical Variable';
   TITLE2 'With Discrete Values';
   VBAR RELIABLE / DISCRETE;
RUN;
```

## SOLUTION TO PROBLEM 5

```
*-------------------------------------------------------------*
| Data set CARS created in PROBLEM 1                           |
*-------------------------------------------------------------*;
PROC CHART DATA=CARS;
   TITLE 'Vertical Bar Chart for a Continuous Numerical Variable';
```

```
***Part A;
   VBAR MILEAGE;
***Part B;
   VBAR MILEAGE / MIDPOINTS=15 to 40 by 5;
***Part C;
   VBAR MILEAGE / LEVELS=5;
RUN;
```

## SOLUTION TO PROBLEM 6

```
DATA BASKETBA;
   INFILE 'C:\WORKBOOK\BASKET.DTA' PAD;
   INPUT @5  GENDER  $1.
         @17 POINTS   2.;
RUN;

PROC CHART DATA=BASKETBA;
   TITLE 'Total Points for Men and Women Basketball Players';
   VBAR GENDER / SUMVAR=POINTS TYPE=SUM;
RUN;
```

## SOLUTION TO PROBLEM 7

```
*--------------------------------------------------------------*
| Data set CARS created in PROBLEM 1                           |
*--------------------------------------------------------------*;
PROC CHART DATA=CARS;
   TITLE 'Reliability by Car Size';
   VBAR RELIABLE / GROUP=SIZE DISCRETE;
RUN;
```

## SOLUTION TO PROBLEM 8

```
*--------------------------------------------------------------*
| Data set CARS created in PROBLEM 1                           |
*--------------------------------------------------------------*;
PROC CHART DATA=CARS;
   TITLE 'Distribution by Manufacturer and Car Size';
   VBAR MANUFACT / SUBGROUP=SIZE;
RUN;
```

## SOLUTION TO PROBLEM 9

```
*--------------------------------------------------------------*
| Data set CARS created in PROBLEM 1                           |
*--------------------------------------------------------------*;
PROC CHART DATA=CARS;
   TITLE 'Three-Dimensional Block Chart';
   BLOCK RELIABLE / GROUP=SIZE SUMVAR=MILEAGE TYPE=MEAN DISCRETE;
   FORMAT MILEAGE 3.;
RUN;
```

# CHAPTER 19 The PLOT Procedure

## SOLUTION TO PROBLEM 1

```
LIBNAME WORKBOOK 'C:\WORKBOOK';
OPTIONS FMTSEARCH=(WORKBOOK) LS=64 PS=48;

PROC PLOT DATA=WORKBOOK.CLINICAL;
   TITLE 'Plots of Blood Pressure versus Heart Rate';
***Part A;
   PLOT SBP*HR;
***Part B;
   PLOT SBP*HR='o';
***Part C;
   PLOT SBP*HR=GENDER;
RUN;
QUIT;
```

## SOLUTION TO PROBLEM 2

```
LIBNAME WORKBOOK 'C:\WORKBOOK';
OPTIONS FMTSEARCH=(WORKBOOK) LS=64 PS=48;

PROC PLOT DATA=WORKBOOK.CLINICAL;
   TITLE 'Plots of Blood Pressure versus Heart Rate';
***Part A;
   PLOT (SBP DBP)*(HR);
***Part B;
   PLOT SBP*HR='S'  DBP*HR='D' / OVERLAY;
RUN;
QUIT;
```

## SOLUTION TO PROBLEM 3

```
LIBNAME WORKBOOK 'C:\WORKBOOK';
OPTIONS FMTSEARCH=(WORKBOOK) LS=64 PS=48;

PROC PLOT DATA=WORKBOOK.CLINICAL;
   TITLE1 'Plots of Blood Pressure versus Heart Rate';
   TITLE2 'Demonstrating the Labelling Feature';
   PLOT SBP*HR $ PRIM_DX='o';
RUN;
QUIT;
```

## SOLUTION TO PROBLEM 4

```
DATA LEAD;
   INPUT LAB $ SUBJECT $ LEVEL_1 LEVEL_2;
   LABEL LEVEL_1 = 'Lead at Time 1'
         LEVEL_2 = 'Lead at Time 2';
DATALINES;
Carter 1 3 3
Carter 2 6 6.5
Carter 3 9 9.5
H&K 1 3.5 3
H&K 2 7 7
H&K 3 10 10
Boston 1 1 2
Boston 2 5 6
Boston 3 7 6
;

OPTIONS LS=64 PS=24 PAGENO=1;
```

```
PROC PLOT DATA=LEAD;
   TITLE 'Lead Levels at Time 1 and Time 2 by Lab and Subject';
   PLOT LEVEL_2 * LEVEL_1 $ LAB = SUBJECT;
RUN;
```

# CHAPTER 20 Efficient Programming

```
*-------------------------------------------*
| Program to create SAS data set EFF1       |
*-------------------------------------------*;
DATA EFF1;
   LENGTH X Y P1 P2 4 GROUP $ 1;
   DO I = 1 TO 10000;
      X  = RANUNI(1357);
      Y  = RANUNI(2468);
      P1 = (X LT .5);
      P2 = (Y LT .001);
      IF X > .8 THEN GROUP = 'A';
      ELSE IF X > .6 THEN GROUP = 'B';
      ELSE IF X > .4 THEN GROUP = 'C';
      ELSE GROUP = 'D';
      OUTPUT;
   END;
   DROP I;
RUN;


*-------------------------------------------*
| Program to create SAS data set EFF2       |
*-------------------------------------------*;
DATA EFF2;
   ARRAY X[100] X1-X100;
   DO I = 1 TO 1000;
      DO J = 1 TO 100;
         X[J] = RANUNI(1357);
      END;
      OUTPUT;
   END;
DROP I J;
RUN;


*-------------------------------------------*
| Program to create data file RAWDATA       |
*-------------------------------------------*;
DATA _NULL_;
   FILE 'C:\WORKBOOK\RAWDATA';
   LENGTH GROUP $ 1;
   ARRAY X[10] X1-X10;
   DO I = 1 TO 10000;
      DO J = 1 TO 10;
         X[J] = RANUNI(1357);
      END;
      IF X1 > .99 THEN GROUP = 'A';
      ELSE GROUP = 'B';
      PUT @1 (X1-X10) (5.3 + 1) @65 GROUP $1.;
   END;
RUN;
```

### SOLUTION TO PROBLEM 1

```
PROC MEANS DATA=EFF1 N MEAN MAXDEC=2;
   TITLE 'Descriptive Statistics on X and Y';
   WHERE P2 = 1;
   VAR X Y;
RUN;
```

### SOLUTION TO PROBLEM 2

```
PROC MEANS DATA=EFF1 N MEAN;
   CLASS GROUP;
RUN;
```

### SOLUTION TO PROBLEM 3

```
PROC SORT DATA=EFF2(WHERE=(X1 > .9)
                    KEEP=X1)
          OUT=SUBSET;
   BY X1;
RUN;
```

### SOLUTION TO PROBLEM 4

```
DATA DESCRIP;
   SET EFF2;
   MEAN = MEAN (OF X1-X100);
   KEEP MEAN;
RUN;
```

### SOLUTION TO PROBLEM 5

```
LIBNAME WORKBOOK 'C:\WORKBOOK';
OPTIONS FMTSEARCH=(WORKBOOK);

DATA _NULL_;
   SET WORKBOOK.CLINICAL;
   FILE PRINT;
   IF SBP > 160 OR DBP > 90 THEN
      PUT ID= SBP= DBP=;
RUN;

 /*--------------------------------------------------------------*
  | Alternative Program: Using a WHERE Data Set Option            |
  | PROC PRINT DATA=WORKBOOK.CLINICAL (WHERE=(SBP GT 160   OR     |
  |                                          DBP GT 90)) ;        |
  |    ID ID;                                                     |
  |    VAR SBP DBP;                                               |
  | RUN;                                                          |
  *--------------------------------------------------------------*/
```

### SOLUTION TO PROBLEM 6

```
DATA SUBSET;
   LENGTH X1-X100 4;
   SET EFF2;
   WHERE X1 > .5;
RUN;
```

### SOLUTION TO PROBLEM 7

```
DATA LONGCHAR;
   LENGTH A B C LETTER $ 1 GROUP $ 7;
   INPUT A B C GROUP;
   LETTER = SUBSTR(GROUP,1,1);
DATALINES;
1 0 1 CONTROL
0 0 0 TREAT
1 1 1 CONTROL
1 0 1 TREAT
0 1 1 TREAT
;
```

### SOLUTION TO PROBLEM 8

```
PROC FORMAT;
   VALUE RANGE 0 - <.2 = 1
              .2 - <.4 = 2
              .4 - <.6 = 3
              .6 - <.8 = 4
              .8 -   1 = 5;
RUN;

PROC FREQ DATA=EFF1;
   TITLE 'Frequencies for X Ranges';
   TABLES X;
   FORMAT X RANGE.;
RUN;
```

### SOLUTION TO PROBLEM 9

```
DATA SUBSET;
*-------------------------------------------------------------*
| You need X1 to compute PROP but do not want it in the data  |
| set SUBSET.  Therefore, you include it in the KEEP= data    |
| set option but do not include it in the KEEP statement.     |
*-------------------------------------------------------------*;
   SET EFF2 (KEEP=X1);
   IF 0 LE X1 LE .5 THEN PROP = 0;
      ELSE PROP = 1;
   KEEP PROP;
RUN;
```

### SOLUTION TO PROBLEM 10

```
*-------------------------------------------------------------*
| On most platforms, the efficient program ran faster (not    |
| counting the time to create the index) than the inefficient |
| program, except on this author's release of SAS (6.10)      |
| running on a 486 computer under Windows 3.1.  You may want  |
| to benchmark programs with and without indexes in your      |
| particular computing environment.                           |
*-------------------------------------------------------------*;
PROC DATASETS LIBRARY=WORK;
   MODIFY EFF1;
   INDEX CREATE P2;
RUN;

PROC FREQ DATA=EFF1;
   TITLE 'Where Processing - Index Used';
   WHERE P2 = 1;
   TABLES GROUP;
RUN;

PROC DATASETS LIBRARY=WORK;
   MODIFY EFF1;
   INDEX DELETE P2;
RUN;
QUIT;
```

### SOLUTION TO PROBLEM 11

```
DATA SUBSET;
   INFILE 'C:\WORKBOOK\RAWDATA'; ***The location of RAWDATA;
   INPUT  @65 GROUP $1. @;
```

```
   IF GROUP = 'A' THEN DO;
      INPUT @1 (X1-X10) (5.3 + 1);
      OUTPUT;
   END;
RUN;
```

### SOLUTION TO PROBLEM 12

```
DATA NEW;
   SET EFF1;
   IF P2 = 0 THEN NEWVAR = Y;
   ELSE NEWVAR = X;
RUN;
```

# CHAPTER 21 Longer and More Advanced Problems

## SOLUTION TO PROBLEM 1

```
*-----------------------------------------------------------*
| Program Name: CLIN_X.SAS   in C:\WORKBOOK                 |
| Purpose: To analyze the CLIN_X data base                  |
*-----------------------------------------------------------*;
***Part A;
OPTIONS PAGENO=1 NOCENTER;

LIBNAME WORKBOOK 'C:\WORKBOOK';
LIBNAME LIBRARY 'C:\WORKBOOK';

*-----------------------------------------------------------*
| Create a permanent FORMAT library in C:\WORKBOOK          |
*-----------------------------------------------------------*;
PROC FORMAT LIBRARY = LIBRARY;
   VALUE $DXCODES '01' = 'Cold'
                  '02' = 'Flu'
                  '03' = 'Break/Fracture'
                  '04' = 'Routine Physical'
                  '05' = 'Heart Problem'
                  '06' = 'Lung Disorder'
                  '07' = 'Abdominal Pain'
                  '08' = 'Laceration'
                  '09' = 'Resp. Infection'
                  '10' = 'Lyme disease'
                  '11' = 'Ear Ache';
   VALUE $RXCODES  '1' = 'Immunization'
                   '2' = 'Casting'
                   '3' = 'Beta Blocker'
                   '4' = 'ACE Inhibitor'
                   '5' = 'Antihistamine'
                   '6' = 'Ibuprofen'
                   '7' = 'Aspirin'
                   '8' = 'Antibiotic';
RUN;

*-----------------------------------------------------------*
| Create a permanent SAS data set called CLIN_X and place it |
| in a subdirectory called C:\WORKBOOK                       |
*-----------------------------------------------------------*;
DATA WORKBOOK.CLIN_X;
   INFILE 'C:\WORKBOOK\CLIN_X.DTA' PAD;
   INPUT   @1  ID      $3.
           @4  VISIT    MMDDYY6.
           @10 DX      $2.
           @12 HR       3.
           @15 SBP      3.
           @18 DBP      3.
           RX_1         $1.
           RX_2         $1.;
FORMAT VISIT MMDDYY8.
       DX $DXCODES.
       RX_1 RX_2 $RXCODES.;
RUN;

***Part B;
*-----------------------------------------------------------*
| Sort by ID and visit date                                 |
*-----------------------------------------------------------*;
```

```
PROC SORT DATA=WORKBOOK.CLIN_X;
   BY ID VISIT;
RUN;

*------------------------------------------------------------*
| Create a data set of LAST visits                           |
*------------------------------------------------------------*;
DATA LAST;
   SET WORKBOOK.CLIN_X;
   BY ID;
   IF LAST.ID;
RUN;

***Part C;
PROC MEANS DATA=LAST N MEAN STD MAXDEC=2;
   TITLE 'Means Based on the Last Visit per Patient';
   VAR HR SBP DBP;
RUN;

***Part D;
*------------------------------------------------------------*
| Use PROC MEANS to create a data set which represents the   |
| mean HR, SBP, and DBP for each patient.                    |
*------------------------------------------------------------*;
PROC MEANS DATA=WORKBOOK.CLIN_X NOPRINT NWAY;
   CLASS ID;
   VAR HR SBP DBP;
   OUTPUT OUT=MEANS MEAN=M_HR M_SBP M_DBP;
RUN;

PROC MEANS DATA=MEANS N MEAN STD MAXDEC=2;
   TITLE 'Means Based on Patient Means';
   VAR M_HR M_SBP M_DBP;
RUN;

***Part E;
*------------------------------------------------------------*
| Compute frequencies for DX, RX_1, and RX_2.  First you need |
| to create an observation for each RX for each patient.     |
*------------------------------------------------------------*;
DATA TREAT;
   SET WORKBOOK.CLIN_X;
   RX = RX_1;
   IF RX NE ' ' THEN OUTPUT;
   RX = RX_2;
   IF RX NE ' ' THEN OUTPUT;
   KEEP ID VISIT RX;
RUN;

PROC FREQ DATA=WORKBOOK.CLIN_X;
   TITLE 'Frequencies of DX codes in CLIN_X';
   TABLES DX /NOCUM;
RUN;

PROC FREQ DATA=TREAT;
   TITLE 'Frequencies of RX codes';
   TABLES RX / NOCUM;
RUN;
```

**SOLUTION TO PROBLEM 2**

```
*-------------------------------------------------------------*
|Program Name: MORSE.SAS  in C:\WORKBOOK                       |
|Purpose: To convert plain text into Morse code and to         |
|         illustrate the use of array boundaries and some      |
|         string functions                                     |
|                                                              |
*-------------------------------------------------------------*;

*-------------------------------------------------------------*
| ARRAY solution                                               |
*-------------------------------------------------------------*;
OPTIONS NOCENTER LS=78 PS=59 NONUMBER NODATE;

DATA _NULL_;
FILE PRINT;
TITLE;

ARRAY M[65:90] $ 4 ('.-' '-...' '-.-.' '-.' '.' '-...' '--.' '....' '..'
                    '.---' '-.-' '.-..' '--' '-.' '---' '.--.' '.--.'
                    '.-.' '...' '-' '..-' '...-' '.--' '-..-' '-.--' '--..');
   INFILE DATALINES;
   LENGTH LETTER $ 1 MORSE $ 4;
   INPUT LINE $80.;
   DO I = 1 TO LENGTH(LINE);
      LETTER = UPCASE(SUBSTR(LINE,I,1));
      IF LETTER EQ ' ' THEN MORSE = ' ';
      ELSE MORSE = M[RANK(LETTER)];
      PUT MORSE @;
   END;
PUT; ***Go to a new line;
DATALINES;
This is a TEST
abcdefg
hijklmn
opqrstu
vwxyz
;
RUN;

*-------------------------------------------------------------*
| INFORMAT solution                                            |
*-------------------------------------------------------------*;
PROC FORMAT;
   INVALUE $CONV (UPCASE)
      'A'='.-'  'B'='-...'  'C'='-.-.'  'D'='-..' 'E'='.'
      'F'='..-.' 'G'='--.' 'H'='....' 'I'='..' 'J'='.---'
      'K'='-.-' 'L'='.-..' 'M'='--' 'N'='-.' 'O'='---'
      'P'='.--.' 'Q'='--.-' 'R'='.-.' 'S'='...' 'T'='-'
      'U'='..-' 'V'='...-' 'W'='.--' 'X'='-..-' 'Y'='-.--'
      'Z'='--..';
RUN;

OPTIONS NONUMBER NODATE;

DATA _NULL_;
   TITLE;
   FILE PRINT;
   LENGTH LETTER $ 4;
   INPUT LINE $80.;
   DO I = 1 TO LENGTH(LINE);
```

```
      LETTER = INPUT(SUBSTR(LINE,I,1),$CONV.);
      PUT LETTER @ ;
   END;
PUT;  ***Go to a new line;
DATALINES;
This is a TEST
abcdefg
hijklmn
opqrstu
vwxyz
;
```

## SOLUTION TO PROBLEM 3

```
LIBNAME WORKBOOK 'C:\WORKBOOK';
OPTIONS FMTSEARCH=(WORKBOOK);

***Part A;
DATA _NULL_;
   SET WORKBOOK.CLINICAL(KEEP=ID DOB VISIT);
   OLD_ID = LAG(ID);
   FILE PRINT;
   IF _N_ = 1 AND ID = ' ' THEN PUT 'The first ID is missing';
   ELSE IF ID = ' ' THEN
      PUT 'ID is missing for the subject following ' OLD_ID;
   IF VISIT LT DOB AND VISIT NE . THEN
      PUT 'Visit date before DOB for ID 'ID
          ':  DOB is ' DOB ' Visit date is ' VISIT;
RUN;

***Part B;
DATA BP_HI_LO;
   SET WORKBOOK.CLINICAL;
   IF 0 LE SBP LT 100   OR
      SBP GT 200        OR
      0 LE DBP LT 50    OR
      DBP GT 180 THEN OUTPUT;
RUN;

PROC PRINT DATA=BP_HI_LO;
   TITLE 'Listing of all Patients with Blood Pressures Out of Range';
RUN;

***Part C;
OPTIONS NODATE NONUMBER;
PROC PRINT DATA=WORKBOOK.CLINICAL LABEL;
   WHERE ((('01MAY96'D - DOB)/365.25) GT 50);
   TITLE1 'Report for All Patients Older than Fifty Years Old';
   TITLE2 '-------------------------------------------------';
   LABEL ID  = 'Subject'
         HR  = 'Heart Rate'
         SBP = 'Systolic Blood Pressure'
         DBP = 'Diastolic Blood Pressure';
   ID ID;
   VAR HR SBP DBP;
RUN;

***Part D;
PROC FREQ DATA=WORKBOOK.CLINICAL;
   TITLE 'Frequencies for Patients with DX 01, 02, or 04';
   WHERE PRIM_DX IN ('01','02','04');
   TABLES GENDER VITAMINS PREGNANT;
RUN;
```

```
***Part E;
DATA PREG_35;
   SET WORKBOOK.CLINICAL(KEEP=ID GENDER VITAMINS DOB
                         WHERE=(GENDER = 'F'));
   AGE = ('01MAY96'D - DOB)/365.35;
   IF AGE GT 35;
   AGE = INT(AGE); ***Truncate AGE after it is compared;
RUN;

PROC PRINT DATA=PREG_35;
   TITLE 'ID and Vitamin Status for Pregnant Women Over 35';
   ID ID;
   VAR AGE VITAMINS;
RUN;
```

# CHAPTER 22 Basic Descriptive Statistics

## SOLUTION TO PROBLEM 1

```
LIBNAME WORKBOOK 'C:\WORKBOOK';

OPTIONS NOCENTER FMTSEARCH=(WORKBOOK);
TITLE 'Problem 1, Chapter 22';

***Run the program in Appendix A to create the SAS data set CLINICAL;

*** Part A;
PROC MEANS DATA=WORKBOOK.CLINICAL N MEAN STD STDERR MAXDEC=3;
   VAR HR SBP DBP;
RUN;

*** Part B;
PROC MEANS DATA=WORKBOOK.CLINICAL N MEAN STD STDERR MAXDEC=3;
   CLASS GENDER;
   VAR HR SBP DBP;
RUN;

 /*-------------------------------------------------------------*
  | Alternative solution to part B:                              |
  |                                                              |
  | PROC SORT DATA=WORKBOOK.CLINICAL;                            |
  |    BY GENDER;                                                |
  | RUN;                                                         |
  |                                                              |
  | PROC MEANS DATA=WORKBOOK.CLINICAL N MEAN STD                 |
  |            STDERR MAXDEC=3;                                  |
  |    BY GENDER;                                                |
  |    VAR HR SBP DBP;                                           |
  | RUN;                                                         |
  *-------------------------------------------------------------*/

*** Part C;
PROC UNIVARIATE DATA=WORKBOOK.CLINICAL;
   VAR HR SBP DBP;
RUN;

*** Part D;
PROC UNIVARIATE DATA=WORKBOOK.CLINICAL NORMAL PLOT;
   VAR SBP;
RUN;

*--------------------------------------------------------------*
| At alpha = .05 we do not reject the null hypothesis that SBP |
| is normally distributed (p = .5997).                         |
*--------------------------------------------------------------*;
```

## SOLUTION TO PROBLEM 2

```
*--------------------------------------------------------------*
| Create a temporary data set called CLIN_AGE  which includes  |
| age at time of visit.                                        |
*--------------------------------------------------------------*;
TITLE 'Problem 2, Chapter 22';

DATA CLIN_AGE;
   SET WORKBOOK.CLINICAL;
   AGE = INT((VISIT - DOB) / 365.25);
```

```
   IF 0 LE AGE LT 65 THEN AGEGROUP = 1;
   ELSE IF AGE GE 65 THEN AGEGROUP = 2;
RUN;

PROC MEANS DATA=CLIN_AGE N MEAN STD MAXDEC=3;
   CLASS GENDER AGEGROUP;
   VAR HR SBP DBP;
RUN;

 /*-----------------------------------------------------------*
  | Alternative Solution:                                      |
  |                                                            |
  | PROC FORMAT;                                               |
  |    VALUE AGEGROUP LOW-<65 = '1'                            |
  |                   65-HIGH = '2';                           |
  | RUN;                                                       |
  |                                                            |
  | DATA CLIN_AGE;                                             |
  |    SET WORKBOOK.CLINICAL;                                  |
  |    AGE = INT((VISIT - DOB) / 365.25);                      |
  | RUN;                                                       |
  |                                                            |
  | PROC MEANS DATA=CLIN_AGE N MEAN STD MAXDEC=3;              |
  |    CLASS GENDER AGE;                                       |
  |    FORMAT AGE AGEGROUP.;                                   |
  |    VAR HR SBP DBP;                                         |
  | RUN;                                                       |
  |                                                            |
  | By applying the AGEGROUP format to the variable AGE in the |
  | procedure, the formatted values of AGE, namely '1' and '2' |
  | will be used as levels of AGE, not the original age values.|
  *-----------------------------------------------------------*/
```

**SOLUTION TO PROBLEM 3**

```
TITLE 'Problem 3, Chapter 22';

*** Part A;
PROC FREQ DATA=WORKBOOK.CLINICAL;
   TABLES GENDER PRIM_DX SEC_DX VITAMINS PREGNANT;
RUN;

*** Part B;
PROC CHART DATA=WORKBOOK.CLINICAL;
   VBAR GENDER PRIM_DX;
RUN;
```

**SOLUTION TO PROBLEM 4**

```
TITLE 'Problem 4, Chapter 22';

*** Part A;
PROC CHART DATA=WORKBOOK.CLINICAL;
   VBAR HR;
RUN;

*** Part B;
PROC CHART DATA=WORKBOOK.CLINICAL;
   VBAR HR / MIDPOINTS = 40 TO 100 BY 10;
RUN;

*** Part C;
PROC CHART DATA=WORKBOOK.CLINICAL;
   VBAR HR / LEVELS = 10;
RUN;
```

**SOLUTION TO PROBLEM 5**

```
TITLE 'Problem 5, Chapter 22';

*---------------------------------------------------------------*
| Even though this problem uses only the variables ID, HR,      |
| SBP, and DBP, the program that follows creates a data set     |
| using all the variables in the raw data as well as formats    |
| and labels.  You may omit this extra baggage if you wish.     |
*---------------------------------------------------------------*;
PROC FORMAT;
   VALUE $DX  '01' = 'Cold'
              '02' = 'Flu'
              '03' = 'Break/Fracture'
              '04' = 'Routine Physical'
              '05' = 'Heart Problem'
              '06' = 'Lung Disorder'
              '07' = 'Abdominal Pain'
              '08' = 'Laceration'
              '09' = 'Resp. Infection'
              '10' = 'Lyme Disease'
              '11' = 'Ear Ache';
   VALUE $RX  '1' = 'Immunization'
              '2' = 'Casting'
              '3' = 'Beta Blocker'
              '4' = 'ACE Inhibitor'
              '5' = 'Antihistamine'
              '6' = 'Ibuprofen'
              '7' = 'Aspirin'
              '8' = 'Antibiotic';
RUN;

DATA CLIN_X;
   INFILE 'C:\WORKBOOK\CLIN_X.DTA' PAD;
   INPUT    @1  ID      $3.
            @4  VISIT    MMDDYY6.
            @10 DX      $2.
            @12 HR        3.
            @15 SBP       3.
            @18 DBP       3.
            RX_1        $1.
            RX_2        $1.;
   FORMAT VISIT MMDDYY8.
          DX $DX.
          RX_1 RX_2 $RX.;
RUN;

*---------------------------------------------------------------*
| Computing the mean for each subject                           |
*---------------------------------------------------------------*;
PROC MEANS NOPRINT NWAY DATA=CLIN_X;
   CLASS ID;
   VAR HR SBP DBP;
   OUTPUT OUT=SUBJMEAN
          MEAN = M_HR M_SBP M_DBP;
RUN;

*---------------------------------------------------------------*
| Computing the mean of the subject means                       |
*---------------------------------------------------------------*;
PROC MEANS DATA=SUBJMEAN N MEAN MAXDEC=3;
   VAR M_HR M_SBP M_DBP;
RUN;
```

```
*-------------------------------------------------------------*
| Use the last visit for each patient.                        |
| Make sure the data set is in ID and visit date order.       |
*-------------------------------------------------------------*;
PROC SORT DATA=CLIN_X;
   BY ID VISIT;
RUN;

DATA LAST;
   SET CLIN_X;
   BY ID;
   IF LAST.ID;
RUN;

PROC MEANS DATA=LAST N MEAN MAXDEC=3;
   VAR HR SBP DBP;
RUN;
```

# CHAPTER 23 Tests of Proportions

## SOLUTION TO PROBLEM 1

```
PROC FORMAT;
   VALUE YESNO 1='YES' 0='NO';
RUN;

DATA CPR;
   INFILE 'C:\WORKBOOK\CPR.DTA';
   INPUT SUBJECT  1-3
         V_FIB     4
         RESP      5
         AGEGROUP  6
         SURVIVE   7;

   LABEL V_FIB    = 'PT IN V-FIB?'
         RESP     = 'PT ON RESPIRATOR?'
         AGEGROUP = 'AGE >= 70?'
         SURVIVE  = 'DID PT SURVIVE?';

   FORMAT V_FIB RESP AGEGROUP SURVIVE YESNO.;

RUN;

*-------------------------------------------------------------*
| Note the use of the double quotes in the following TITLE    |
| statement.  This is one way to allow the single quote in the |
| word Fisher's.                                               |
*-------------------------------------------------------------*;
PROC FREQ DATA=CPR;
   TITLE "Two-way tables with Fisher's Exact Test and Chi-square";
   TABLES (V_FIB RESP AGEGROUP)*SURVIVE / CHISQ;
RUN;
```

## SOLUTION TO PROBLEM 2

```
DATA COUNTS;
   INPUT GENDER $ CANDID $ COUNT;
DATALINES;
M A 35
F A 45
M B 70
F B 50
;
PROC FREQ;
   TITLE 'Chi-square Based on Frequency Data';
   TABLES CANDID*GENDER / CHISQ;
   WEIGHT COUNT;
RUN;
```

## SOLUTION TO PROBLEM 3

```
LIBNAME WORKBOOK 'C:\WORKBOOK';
OPTIONS FMTSEARCH=(WORKBOOK);


*** Part A;
PROC FORMAT;
   VALUE $GENDER 'M' = 'MALE'
                 'F' = 'FEMALE';
   VALUE $YESNO  '0' = 'NO'
                 '1' = 'YES';
RUN;
```

```
PROC FREQ DATA=WORKBOOK.CLINICAL;
   TITLE 'Two-way Tables';
   TABLES VITAMINS*GENDER / CHISQ;
   FORMAT GENDER $GENDER.
          VITAMINS $YESNO.;
RUN;

*-------------------------------------------------------------*
| Using either the Fisher's exact test or the continuity      |
| corrected Chi-square, do not reject the null hypothesis that |
| there is no relationship between vitamin use and gender.    |
*-------------------------------------------------------------*;

*** Part B;
PROC FREQ DATA=WORKBOOK.CLINICAL;
   TABLES VITAMINS*(GENDER PRIM_DX);
RUN;

*** Part C;
PROC FREQ DATA=WORKBOOK.CLINICAL;
   WHERE GENDER = 'F';
   TABLES VITAMINS*PREGNANT / CHISQ;
RUN;

*-------------------------------------------------------------*
| Using Fisher's exact test (2-tailed), the p-value is .620,  |
| so we do not reject the null hypothesis.                    |
*-------------------------------------------------------------*;
```

**SOLUTION TO PROBLEM 4**

```
DATA MANYCHI;
   TABLE + 1; ***Generate a table identifier;
   DO COLUMN = 'Col 1','Col 2';
      DO ROW = 'Row 1','Row 2';
         INPUT COUNT @;
         OUTPUT;
      END;
   END;
DATALINES;
10 20 30 40
20 25 30 35
200 250 300 350
;
PROC FREQ DATA=MANYCHI;
   TITLE 'Computing Chi-square for Several Tables';
   BY TABLE NOTSORTED; ***Some versions may require the
                         NOTSORTED option;
   TABLES COLUMN*ROW / CHISQ;
   WEIGHT COUNT;
RUN;

/*-----------------------------------------------------------*
 | Alternative program: Using a 3-way table instead of        |
 |                      a BY statement                        |
 |                                                            |
 | PROC FREQ DATA=MANYCHI;                                    |
 |    TITLE 'Computing Chi-square for Several Tables';        |
 |    TABLES TABLE*COLUMN*ROW / CHISQ;                        |
 |    WEIGHT COUNT;                                           |
 | RUN;                                                       |
 *-----------------------------------------------------------*/
```

### SOLUTION TO PROBLEM 5

```
DATA CARS;
INFILE 'C:\WORKBOOK\CARS.DTA' PAD;
INPUT  @ 1 SIZE      $9.
       @50 RELIABLE  1.;
IF 0 LE RELIABLE LT 3 THEN GROUP = 'Below 3';
ELSE IF RELIABLE GE 3 THEN GROUP = 'Above 3';
RUN;

PROC FREQ DATA=CARS;
   TITLE 'Chi-square for a 2 X 3 Table';
   TABLES GROUP*SIZE / CHISQ;
RUN;
```

### SOLUTION TO PROBLEM 6

```
*---------------------------------------------------------------*
| PROC FREQ (Release 6.10 and above) solution                   |
*---------------------------------------------------------------*;
DATA MCNEMAR;
   INPUT SUBJECT $ BEFORE $ AFTER $;
DATALINES;
 1 Anti   Anti
 2 Anti   Pro
 3 Pro    Anti
 4 Pro    Anti
 5 Pro    Pro
 6 Anti   Pro
 7 Pro    Anti
 8 Pro    Anti
 9 Pro    Anti
10 Pro    Anti
;
PROC FREQ DATA=MCNEMAR;
   TITLE "Computing McNemar's Test";
   TABLES AFTER*BEFORE / AGREE; ***Note, Release 6.10 and higher;
RUN;

*---------------------------------------------------------------*
| DATA step solution for those using versions prior to 6.10     |
*---------------------------------------------------------------*;
DATA MCNEMAR;
   INPUT SUBJECT $ BEFORE $ AFTER $;
DATALINES;
 1 Anti   Anti
 2 Anti   Pro
 3 Pro    Anti
 4 Pro    Anti
 5 Pro    Pro
 6 Anti   Pro
 7 Pro    Anti
 8 Pro    Anti
 9 Pro    Anti
10 Pro    Anti
;
PROC FREQ DATA=MCNEMAR;
   TABLES AFTER*BEFORE / NOPRINT OUT=COUNTS;
RUN;

DATA _NULL_;
   FILE PRINT;
   SET COUNTS;
```

```
   IF AFTER NE BEFORE; ***Select only discordant cells;
   B = LAG (COUNT);
   C = COUNT;
   IF  _N_ = 3 THEN DO; ***Just one way of many ways to do this;
      MCNEMAR = (B - C)**2 / (B + C);
      PROBCHI = (1 - PROBCHI(MCNEMAR,1));
      MCNEMARC = (ABS(B-C)-1)**2 / (B + C);
      PROBCHIC = (1 - PROBCHI(MCNEMARC,1));
      FORMAT MCNEMAR MCNEMARC 8.3 PROBCHI PROBCHIC 8.4;
      PUT 'Uncorrected McNemar Chisquare = ' MCNEMAR ' Prob = ' PROBCHI /
          'Corrected McNemar Chisquare   = ' MCNEMARC ' Prob = '  PROBCHIC;
   END;
RUN;
```

**SOLUTION TO PROBLEM 7**

```
DATA COUNTS;
   INPUT BEFORE $ AFTER $ COUNT;
DATALINES;
Anti Anti 70
Anti Pro  10
Pro Anti  4
Pro Pro   50
;
PROC FREQ DATA=COUNTS;
   TITLE "Computing McNemar's Test - Using Frequency Counts";
   TABLES AFTER*BEFORE / AGREE; ***Note, version 6.10 and higher;
   WEIGHT COUNT;
RUN;
```

# CHAPTER 24 Comparing Means: Two Groups

**SOLUTION TO PROBLEM 1**

```
LIBNAME WORKBOOK 'C:\WORKBOOK';
OPTIONS FMTSEARCH=(WORKBOOK);

PROC TTEST DATA=WORKBOOK.CLINICAL;
   TITLE 'Unpaired T-test';
   CLASS VITAMINS;
   VAR HR SBP DBP;
RUN;
```

**SOLUTION TO PROBLEM 2**

```
DATA TWOWAY2;
   LENGTH GROUP $ 1;
   INPUT GROUP $ CHOL HDL TRIG;
DATALINES;
A 220 45 120
A 180 60 70
A 240 75 100
A 285 50 150
A 288 55 102
A 302 70 130
B 155 40 130
B 120 30 170
B 112 35 160
B 126 35 120
B 133 48 80
;
PROC TTEST DATA=TWOWAY2;
   TITLE 'Unpaired T-test';
   CLASS GROUP;
   VAR CHOL HDL TRIG;
RUN;

*-------------------------------------------------------------*
| The assumption of equal variance is not rejected for any of  |
| the three variables, although you come close to rejecting it |
| for CHOL. In any event, both of the p-values (equal or       |
| unequal variance assumptions) for the CHOL comparison are    |
| highly significant.                                          |
*-------------------------------------------------------------*;
```

**SOLUTION TO PROBLEM 3**

```
DATA TWOWAY3;
   INPUT DIET $ WEIGHT @@;
DATALINES;
1 45 1 48 1 57 1 73 1 63
2 80 2 72 2 130 2 65 2 220 2 200
;
PROC NPAR1WAY DATA=TWOWAY3 WILCOXON;
   TITLE 'Wilcoxon Rank Sum Test';
   CLASS DIET;
   VAR WEIGHT;
RUN;

*-------------------------------------------------------------*
| Consulting a Wilcoxon Rank Sum table, the critical values    |
| for p = .05 are (18,42), for p = .02 (17,43), and for p=.01  |
| (16,44).  Since the sum of ranks for Diet 1 is 17, you can   |
| use p = .02 for this test.  The normal approximation value   |
| of .0225 is very close to this value.                        |
*-------------------------------------------------------------*;
```

### SOLUTION TO PROBLEM 4

```
DATA TWOWAY4;
   INPUT SUBJECT SBP_P SBP_D DBP_P DBP_D;
   DIFF_SBP = SBP_D - SBP_P;
   DIFF_DBP = DBP_D - DBP_P;

   ***Note: The labels are not required in this solution;
   LABEL SBP_P = 'SBP Placebo'
         SBP_D = 'SBP Drug'
         DBP_P = 'DBP Placebo'
         DBP_D = 'DBP Drug'
         DIFF_SBP = 'SBP Drug - SBP Placebo'
         DIFF_DBP = 'DBP Drug - DBP Placebo';
DATALINES;
1 180 160 90 80
2 220 170 110 96
3 190 140 88 78
4 182 142 108 84
5 160 154 88 86
6 190 182 88 82
;
PROC MEANS DATA=TWOWAY4 N MEAN STD STDERR T PRT MAXDEC=3;
   TITLE 'Unpaired T-test';
   VAR DIFF_SBP DIFF_DBP;
RUN;
```

### SOLUTION TO PROBLEM 5

```
PROC UNIVARIATE DATA=TWOWAY4;
   TITLE 'Wilcoxon Signed Rank Test';
   VAR DIFF_SBP DIFF_DBP;
RUN;

*-------------------------------------------------------------*
| Both variables are significantly different just as they were |
| with a paired t-test.  However, the p-values are slightly    |
| larger (p = .03 for both) compared to values of less than    |
| .02 for the paired t-tests.                                  |
*-------------------------------------------------------------*;
```

### SOLUTION TO PROBLEM 6

```
DATA TWOWAY6;
   INFILE 'C:\WORKBOOK\CLIN_X.DTA' PAD;
   INPUT @1  ID      $3.
         @4  VISIT   MMDDYY6.
         @12 HR      3.
         @15 SBP     3.;
   FORMAT VISIT MMDDYY8.;
RUN;

PROC SORT DATA=TWOWAY6;
   BY ID VISIT;
RUN;

DATA VISIT_2;
   SET TWOWAY6;
   BY ID;

*-------------------------------------------------------------*
| Select the first and last visit for all patients with two or |
| more visits.  FIRST.ID and LAST.ID will be equal if there is |
| only one visit (both=1) or if it is not the first or last    |
| visit (both=0) for patients with more than two visits.       |
*-------------------------------------------------------------*;
```

```
   IF FIRST.ID EQ LAST.ID THEN DELETE;
RUN;

DATA PAIRED;
   SET VISIT_2;
      BY ID;
   DIFF_HR = DIF(HR); ***Alternative DIFF_HR = HR - LAG(HR);
   DIFF_SBP = dif(SBP);
   IF LAST.ID THEN OUTPUT;

   LABEL DIFF_HR  = 'HR Last Visit - HR First Visit'
         DIFF_SBP = 'SBP Last Visit - SBP First Visit';
   KEEP DIFF_HR DIFF_SBP;
RUN;

PROC MEANS DATA=PAIRED N MEAN STD STDERR T PRT;
   TITLE 'Paired T-test Example with Longitudinal Data';
   VAR DIFF_HR DIFF_SBP;
RUN;
```

# CHAPTER 25 Analysis of Variance

### SOLUTION TO PROBLEM 1

```
OPTIONS NOCENTER PAGENO=1 PS=59 LS=78;

DATA TOMATO;
   INPUT FERT $ WEIGHT;
DATALINES;
5-10-5   .85
5-10-5   .88
5-10-5   .87
5-10-5   .83
5-10-10  .92
5-10-10  .97
5-10-10  .86
5-10-10  .88
20-5-5   .64
20-5-5   .50
20-5-5   .48
20-5-5   .42
;
PROC ANOVA DATA=TOMATO;
   TITLE 'One-way ANOVA on Tomato Data';
   CLASS FERT;
   MODEL WEIGHT = FERT;
   MEANS FERT / SNK;
RUN;
QUIT;
```

### SOLUTION TO PROBLEM 2

```
*------------------------------------------------------------*
| You can use a previously saved SAS data set if you wish.    |
| If you read the raw data file as in this example, you only  |
| need to read in the SIZE and MILEAGE values.                |
*------------------------------------------------------------*;
DATA CARS;
   INFILE 'C:\WORKBOOK\CARS.DTA' PAD;
   INPUT SIZE    $ 1-9
         MILEAGE   38-39;
RUN;

PROC ANOVA DATA=CARS;
   TITLE 'Comparing Car Mileages as a Function of Car Size';
   CLASS SIZE;
   MODEL MILEAGE = SIZE;
   MEANS SIZE / DUNCAN;
   MEANS SIZE / SCHEFFE ALPHA=.10;
RUN;
QUIT;
```

### SOLUTION TO PROBLEM 3

```
DATA HYPER;
   INPUT GROUP $ DRUG $ ACTIVITY;
DATALINES;
ADD      PLACEBO  90
ADD      PLACEBO  88
ADD      PLACEBO  95
CONTROL  PLACEBO  60
CONTROL  PLACEBO  62
CONTROL  PLACEBO  66
```

```
ADD      RITALIN  72
ADD      RITALIN  70
ADD      RITALIN  64
CONTROL  RITALIN  86
CONTROL  RITALIN  86
CONTROL  RITALIN  82
;
***Part A;
PROC ANOVA DATA=HYPER;
   TITLE 'One-Way ANOVA with ADD Data';
   CLASS GROUP DRUG;
   MODEL ACTIVITY = GROUP | DRUG;
   MEANS GROUP|DRUG / DUNCAN;
RUN;
QUIT;

PROC MEANS DATA=HYPER NOPRINT NWAY;
   CLASS GROUP DRUG;
   VAR ACTIVITY;
   OUTPUT OUT=INTERACT MEAN=;
RUN;

PROC PLOT DATA=INTERACT;
   TITLE 'Interaction Plot';
   PLOT ACTIVITY * DRUG = GROUP;
RUN;
QUIT;

***Part B;
PROC SORT DATA=HYPER;
   BY GROUP;
RUN;

PROC TTEST DATA=HYPER;
   TITLE 'T-Test for each Group Separately';
   BY GROUP;
   CLASS DRUG;
   VAR ACTIVITY;
RUN;

***Part C;
DATA ONEWAY;
   SET HYPER;
   LENGTH COND $ 15;
   COND = COMPRESS(GROUP||'-'||DRUG);
   KEEP ACTIVITY COND;
RUN;

PROC ANOVA DATA=ONEWAY;
   TITLE 'One-way ANOVA on Combinations of DRUG and GROUP';
   CLASS COND;
   MODEL ACTIVITY = COND;
   MEANS COND / DUNCAN;
RUN;
QUIT;
```

**SOLUTION TO PROBLEM 4**

```
LIBNAME WORKBOOK 'C:\WORKBOOK';
OPTIONS FMTSEARCH=(WORKBOOK);
```

```
PROC GLM DATA=WORKBOOK.CLINICAL;
   TITLE 'Two-way Unbalanced ANOVA';
   CLASS GENDER VITAMINS;
   MODEL SBP = GENDER | VITAMINS;
   LSMEANS GENDER | VITAMINS;
RUN;
QUIT;
```

### SOLUTION TO PROBLEM 5

```
OPTIONS NOCENTER PAGENO=1 PS=59 LS=78;

***Straightforward DATA step;
DATA CURE;
   LENGTH DRUG GENDER $ 1 DOSE $ 4;
   INPUT DRUG $ GENDER $ DOSE $ TIME;
DATALINES;
A       M       Low       22
A       M      High       20
A       F       Low       18
A       F      High       16
B       M       Low       38
B       M      High       34
B       F       Low       34
B       F      High       30
A       M       Low       21
A       M      High       18
A       F       Low       17
A       F      High       14
B       M       Low       37
B       M      High       33
B       F       Low       34
B       F      High       29
;

***Interesting exercise DATA step;
DATA CURE;
   DO DRUG = 'A','B';
      DO GENDER = 'M','F';
         DO DOSE = 'LOW ','HIGH';
            INPUT CURETIME @@;
            OUTPUT;
         END;
      END;
   END;
DATALINES;
22 20 18 16 38 34 34 30
21 18 17 14 37 33 34 29
;
PROC ANOVA DATA=CURE;
   TITLE 'Three-way Factorial Balanced Design';
   CLASS DRUG GENDER DOSE;
   MODEL CURETIME = DRUG|GENDER|DOSE;
   MEANS DRUG|GENDER|DOSE;
RUN;
QUIT;
```

### SOLUTION TO PROBLEM 6

```
DATA SPELLING;
   DO GENDER = 'Boys ','Girls';
      DO I = 1 to 4;
         DO GRADE = 3,4;
            DO METHOD = 'Phonetic','Memory  ';
               INPUT CORRECT @;
```

```
               OUTPUT;
            END;
         END;
      END;
   END;
DATALINES;
35 30 45 40
37  . 48 42
34 37 47 41
34 29 44 39
37 32 44 42
39 38 50  .
37 38 49 44
36 39 45 40
;
PROC GLM DATA=SPELLING;
   TITLE 'Comparing different Genders, Grades, and Spelling Methods';
   CLASS GENDER GRADE METHOD;
   MODEL CORRECT = GENDER | GRADE | METHOD;
   LSMEANS GENDER | GRADE | METHOD;
RUN;
QUIT;
```

## SOLUTION TO PROBLEM 7

```
DATA REPEAT1;
   LENGTH LEVEL $ 6;
   INPUT SUBJECT LEVEL $ NUMBER @@;
DATALINES;
1 NONE 20 1 MEDIUM 15 1 HIGH  8
2 NONE 10 2 MEDIUM  8 2 HIGH  4
3 NONE 35 3 MEDIUM 25 3 HIGH 23
4 NONE  9 4 MEDIUM  5 4 HIGH  2
5 NONE 28 5 MEDIUM 24 5 HIGH 20
;
PROC ANOVA DATA=REPEAT1;
   TITLE 'A One-Way Repeated Measures Design';
   CLASS SUBJECT LEVEL;
   MODEL NUMBER = SUBJECT LEVEL;
   MEANS LEVEL / SNK;
RUN;
QUIT;

 /*----------------------------------------------------------*
  | Alternative method that uses the REPEATED statement of   |
  | PROC ANOVA.  However, the SNK multiple comparison test   |
  | cannot be performed.  Contrasts will have to be run to   |
  | test pairwise differences.                               |
  *----------------------------------------------------------*/
DATA REPEAT1;
   INPUT SUBJECT N_NONE N_MEDIUM N_HIGH;
DATALINES;
1 20 15  8
2 10  8  4
3 35 25 23
4  9  5  2
5 28 24 20
;
PROC ANOVA DATA=REPEAT1;
   TITLE 'Using the REPEATED Statement of PROC ANOVA';
   MODEL N_NONE N_MEDIUM N_HIGH =  / NOUNI;
   REPEATED LEVEL 3;
RUN;
QUIT;
```

```
 /*-----------------------------------------------------------*
  | The same procedure as above except with contrasts to      |
  | determine pairwise differences.  Note that these contrasts |
  | are computed without any protection or adjustment for a    |
  | type I error.                                              |
  *-----------------------------------------------------------*/
PROC ANOVA DATA=REPEAT1;
   TITLE 'Using the REPEATED Statement of PROC ANOVA';
   MODEL N_NONE N_MEDIUM N_HIGH =  / NOUNI;
   REPEATED LEVEL 3 CONTRAST(1) / NOM SUMMARY;
   REPEATED LEVEL 3 CONTRAST(2) / NOM SUMMARY;
RUN;
QUIT;

 /*-------------------------------------------------------*
  | If this model were run, ignoring the repeated nature of |
  | the model, a simple one-way ANOVA would be run, without |
  | including SUBJECT in the model like this:               |
  | *** Note: INCORRECT Program for Example Only ***        |
  *-------------------------------------------------------*/
DATA REPEAT1;
   LENGTH LEVEL $ 6;
   INPUT SUBJECT LEVEL $ NUMBER @@;
DATALINES;
1 NONE 20 1 MEDIUM 15 1 HIGH  8
2 NONE 10 2 MEDIUM  8 2 HIGH  4
3 NONE 35 3 MEDIUM 25 3 HIGH 23
4 NONE  9 4 MEDIUM  5 4 HIGH  2
5 NONE 28 5 MEDIUM 24 5 HIGH 20
;
PROC ANOVA DATA=REPEAT1;
   TITLE 'A One-Way Repeated Measures Design';
   CLASS LEVEL;
   MODEL NUMBER = LEVEL;
   MEANS LEVEL / SNK;
RUN;
QUIT;
```

### SOLUTION TO PROBLEM 8

```
DATA REPEAT2;
   DO SUBJECT = 1 TO 6;
      IF SUBJECT LE 3 THEN GENDER='Male  ';
      ELSE GENDER = 'Female';

***Note: Precede 'Control' with a blank below so that the levels
         will be plotted in the proper order on the interaction plot;

      DO COND = ' Control','1 oz.','3 oz.';
         INPUT REACT @;
         OUTPUT;
      END;
   END;
DATALINES;
.4 .9 1.2
.6 .6 .8
.8 1.1 1.3
.9 1.1 1.4
1.0 1.5 2.0
.8 1.0 1.6
;
```

```
PROC ANOVA DATA=REPEAT2;
   TITLE 'Two-way ANOVA with a Repeated Measure on One Factor';
   CLASS SUBJECT GENDER COND;
   MODEL REACT = GENDER SUBJECT(GENDER)
                 COND COND*GENDER COND*SUBJECT(GENDER);
   TEST H=GENDER                 E=SUBJECT(GENDER);
   TEST H=COND COND*GENDER       E=COND*SUBJECT(GENDER);
   MEANS GENDER;
   MEANS COND COND*GENDER / DUNCAN E=COND*SUBJECT(GENDER);
RUN;
QUIT;

***Interaction Plot;
PROC MEANS DATA=REPEAT2 NWAY NOPRINT;
   CLASS GENDER COND;
   VAR REACT;
   OUTPUT OUT=INTERACT MEAN=;
RUN;

PROC PLOT DATA=INTERACT;
   TITLE 'Interaction Plot';
   PLOT REACT * COND = GENDER;
RUN;
QUIT;
```

## SOLUTION TO PROBLEM 9

```
*-----------------------------------------------------------*
| Solution without using the REPEATED statement of PROC ANOVA |
*-----------------------------------------------------------*;
DATA TRACK;
   DO RUNNER = 1 TO 4;
      DO TRACK = 'Cinder','Rubber';
         DO BRAND = 'A','B';
            INPUT TIME @;
            OUTPUT;
         END;
      END;
   END;
DATALINES;
11.4 11.5 10.9 10.9
10.8 10.7 10.2 10.0
10.9 11.1 10.7 10.4
10.4 11.2 10.5 10.7
;
*-----------------------------------------------------------*
| An alternative program could have been simply to            |
| read in RUNNER, TRACK, BRAND, and TIME as raw data          |
*-----------------------------------------------------------*;
PROC ANOVA DATA=TRACK;
   TITLE 'Two-way repeated measures model with both factors repeated';
   CLASS RUNNER TRACK BRAND;
   MODEL TIME = RUNNER|TRACK|BRAND;
   MEANS TRACK|BRAND; ***No need for post hoc tests since there
                         are only two levels of each factor;
   TEST H = TRACK             E = RUNNER*TRACK;
   TEST H = BRAND             E = RUNNER*BRAND;
   TEST H = TRACK*BRAND       E = RUNNER*TRACK*BRAND;
RUN;
QUIT;

*-----------------------------------------------------------*
| The same problem using the REPEATED statement of PROC ANOVA |
*-----------------------------------------------------------*;
```

```
DATA TRACK_R;
   INPUT TIME_C_A TIME_C_B TIME_R_A TIME_R_B;
DATALINES;
11.4 11.5 10.9 10.9
10.8 10.7 10.2 10.0
10.9 11.1 10.7 10.4
10.4 11.2 10.5 10.7
;
PROC ANOVA DATA=TRACK_R;
   TITLE 'Two-way repeated measures model with both factors repeated';
   MODEL TIME_C_A TIME_C_B TIME_R_A TIME_R_B = / NOUNI;
   REPEATED TRACK 2 , BRAND 2  / NOM;
RUN;
QUIT;
```

**SOLUTION TO PROBLEM 10**

```
DATA PUZZLE;
   LENGTH SCHOOL $ 13;
   DO AGE = 3 TO 4;
      DO SCHOOL = 'Pre-school','No Pre-school';
         DO N = 1 TO 3;
            SUBJECT + 1;
            DO TRIAL = 1 TO 3;
               INPUT TIME @;
               OUTPUT;
            END;
         END;
      END;
   END;
DROP N;
DATALINES;
52 48 46
51 47 45
53 49 47
60 58 56
59 57 55
61 59 57
45 40 30
44 38 27
46 41 32
52 48 40
51 47 39
53 49 41
;
PROC ANOVA DATA=PUZZLE;
   TITLE 'Three-way ANOVA with One Repeated Measures Factor';
   CLASS SUBJECT SCHOOL AGE TRIAL;
   MODEL TIME = AGE
                SCHOOL
                AGE*SCHOOL       SUBJECT(AGE SCHOOL)
                TRIAL
                TRIAL*AGE
                TRIAL*SCHOOL
                TRIAL*AGE*SCHOOL TRIAL*SUBJECT(AGE SCHOOL);
   TEST H = AGE SCHOOL AGE*SCHOOL
        E = SUBJECT(AGE SCHOOL);
   TEST H = TRIAL TRIAL*AGE TRIAL*SCHOOL TRIAL*AGE*SCHOOL
        E = TRIAL*SUBJECT(AGE SCHOOL);
   MEANS AGE | SCHOOL | TRIAL;
   MEANS TRIAL / SNK E = TRIAL*SUBJECT(AGE SCHOOL);
RUN;
QUIT;
```

**SOLUTION TO PROBLEM 11**

```
DATA LICENSE;
   DO GROUP = 'Yes','No ';
      DO N = 1 TO 4;
         SUBJECT + 1;
         DO COLOR = 'White on Blue   ','Blue on White   ','Black on Yellow';
            DO FONT = 'Helv ','Times';
               INPUT CORRECT @;
               OUTPUT;
            END;
         END;
      END;
   END;
   DROP N;
DATALINES;
21  25  22  23  18  19
21  25  23  24  22  24
24  22  25  20  19  21
27  20  25  18  20  20
19  21  20  21  17  16
21  21  22  22  20  20
20  20  24  18  17  19
24  19  25  17  20  18
;
PROC ANOVA DATA=LICENSE;
   TITLE 'Three-way ANOVA with Repeated Measures on Two Factors';
   CLASS SUBJECT GROUP COLOR FONT;
   MODEL CORRECT = GROUP              SUBJECT(GROUP)
                   COLOR
                   GROUP*COLOR        COLOR*SUBJECT(GROUP)
                   FONT
                   GROUP*FONT         FONT*SUBJECT(GROUP)
                   COLOR*FONT
                   GROUP*COLOR*FONT   COLOR*FONT*SUBJECT(GROUP);
   TEST H = GROUP
        E = SUBJECT(GROUP);
   TEST H = COLOR GROUP*COLOR
        E = COLOR*SUBJECT(GROUP);
   TEST H = FONT GROUP*FONT
        E = FONT*SUBJECT(GROUP);
   TEST H = COLOR*FONT GROUP*COLOR*FONT
        E = COLOR*FONT*SUBJECT(GROUP);
   MEANS GROUP|COLOR|FONT;
   MEANS COLOR / SNK  E = COLOR*SUBJECT(GROUP);
RUN;
QUIT;

*-------------------------------------------------------------*
| Alternate method using the REPEATED statement              |
*-------------------------------------------------------------*;
DATA LICENSER;
INPUT GROUP $ CORRECT1-CORRECT6;
DATALINES;
Police 21  25  22  23  18  19
Police 21  25  23  24  22  24
Police 24  22  25  20  19  21
Police 27  20  25  18  20  20
Lay    19  21  20  21  17  16
Lay    21  21  22  22  20  20
Lay    20  20  24  18  17  19
Lay    24  19  25  17  20  18
;
```

```
PROC ANOVA DATA=LICENSER;
   TITLE 'Three-way ANOVA with Repeated Measures on Two Factors';
   CLASS GROUP;
   MODEL CORRECT1-CORRECT6 = GROUP / NOUNI;
   REPEATED COLOR 3, FONT 2;
   MEANS GROUP;
RUN;
QUIT;
```

**SOLUTION TO PROBLEM 12**

```
DATA TREAD;
   INPUT SUBJ @;
   DO DRUG = 'A','B';
      DO TIME_DAY = 'MORNING','NIGHT  ';
         DO TRIAL = 1 TO 3;
            INPUT SECONDS @;
            OUTPUT;
         END;
      END;
   END;
DATALINES;
1  8   7   9  10  12  13  12  13  15  15  17  16
2  9  10  11  12  13  14  15  16  17  18  19  20
3  7   7   9   9   8  10   9   9  11  11  13  15
4  8   9   9   8   9   9   9  10  10  10  11  12
5  8   8  11   8   9  12  10  12  14  10  13  15
;
PROC ANOVA DATA=TREAD;
   TITLE 'Three-way ANOVA with Repeated Measures on All Factors';
   CLASS SUBJ DRUG TIME_DAY TRIAL;
   MODEL SECONDS = SUBJ|DRUG|TIME_DAY|TRIAL;
   TEST H = DRUG                  E = SUBJ*DRUG;
   TEST H = TIME_DAY              E = SUBJ*TIME_DAY;
   TEST H = TRIAL                 E = SUBJ*TIME_DAY;
   TEST H = DRUG*TIME_DAY         E = SUBJ*DRUG*TIME_DAY;
   TEST H = DRUG*TRIAL            E = SUBJ*DRUG*TRIAL;
   TEST H = TIME_DAY*TRIAL        E = SUBJ*TIME_DAY*TRIAL;
   TEST H = DRUG*TIME_DAY*TRIAL   E = SUBJ*DRUG*TIME_DAY*TRIAL;
MEANS DRUG|TIME_DAY|TRIAL;
MEANS TRIAL / SNK  E = SUBJ*TRIAL;
RUN;
QUIT;
```

# CHAPTER 26

# Parametric and Nonparametric Correlations

## SOLUTION TO PROBLEM 1

```
LIBNAME WORKBOOK 'C:\WORKBOOK';
OPTIONS FMTSEARCH=(WORKBOOK);

PROC CORR DATA=WORKBOOK.CLINICAL NOSIMPLE;
   TITLE 'Simple Correlation Matrix';
   VAR HR SBP DBP;
RUN;
```

## SOLUTION TO PROBLEM 2

```
DATA ITEMS;
   INPUT @1  ID  $3.
         @5  (ITEM1-ITEM10)(1.);
   RAW = SUM (OF ITEM1-ITEM10);
DATALINES;
001 1101111011
002 1111111111
003 1110101010
004 0001010001
005 1110101010
006 0101010101
007 1111111011
008 1110111011
009 0001000100
010 1111011110
;
PROC CORR DATA=ITEMS NOSIMPLE;
   TITLE 'Item and Test Analysis';
   VAR ITEM1-ITEM10;
   WITH RAW;
RUN;

PROC CORR DATA=ITEMS NOSIMPLE ALPHA NOCORR;
   TITLE "Cronbach's Coefficient Alpha";
   VAR ITEM1-ITEM10;
RUN;
```

## SOLUTION TO PROBLEM 3

```
DATA SPEAR;
   INPUT X Y Z;
DATALINES;
1     5     3
2     5     8
5     4    11
4     9    15
5    18    13
20   25    55
;
PROC CORR DATA=SPEAR NOSIMPLE PEARSON SPEARMAN;
   TITLE 'Pearson and Spearman Correlations';
   VAR X Y Z;
RUN;

***Want to make smaller plots;
OPTIONS PS=24 LS=64;

PROC PLOT DATA=SPEAR;
   TITLE 'Scatter plots';
   PLOT X*Y='o'  X*Z='o' Y*Z='o';
RUN;
```

```
***Put options back to original;
OPTIONS PS=59 LS=78;
```

## SOLUTION TO PROBLEM 4

```
*-----------------------------------------------------------------*
| Data set SPEAR created in Problem 3                             |
*-----------------------------------------------------------------*;
PROC RANK DATA=SPEAR OUT=RANKXYZ;
   VAR X Y Z;
   RANKS RANK_X RANK_Y RANK_Z; *These variables hold the
                                Rank values;
RUN;

PROC CORR NOSIMPLE DATA=RANKXYZ;
   TITLE 'Correlating the Ranks of X,Y, and Z';
   VAR RANK_X RANK_Y RANK_Z;
RUN;
```

## CHAPTER 27 Simple, Multiple, and Logistic Regression

### SOLUTION TO PROBLEM 1

```
LIBNAME WORKBOOK 'C:\WORKBOOK';
OPTIONS FMTSEARCH=(WORKBOOK);

PROC REG DATA=WORKBOOK.CLINICAL;
   TITLE 'Simple Linear Regression and Associated Plots';
   MODEL SBP = DBP;
   PLOT SBP*DBP PREDICTED.*DBP='o' / OVERLAY;
   PLOT RESIDUAL.*DBP;
RUN;
QUIT;

*-----------------------------------------------------------*
| The slope is 1.29 and the intercept is 27.65 (rounded).   |
*-----------------------------------------------------------*;
```

### SOLUTION TO PROBLEM 2

```
LIBNAME WORKBOOK 'C:\WORKBOOK';
OPTIONS FMTSEARCH=(WORKBOOK);

PROC REG DATA=WORKBOOK.CLINICAL;
   TITLE 'Plotting Two Types of Confidence Intervals';
   MODEL SBP = DBP;
   PLOT PREDICTED.*DBP='o'
        L95.*DBP='-'
        U95.*DBP='-'
        L95M.*DBP='='
        U95M.*DBP='=' / OVERLAY;
RUN;
QUIT;
```

### SOLUTION TO PROBLEM 3

```
DATA PREDICT;
   INPUT X Y @@;

*-----------------------------------------------------------*
| Two extra data points X=10, Y=., and X=20, Y=., are       |
| included in the data so that predicted values of Y        |
| can be computed.                                          |
*-----------------------------------------------------------*;
DATALINES;
1 4 2 7 5 12 7 15 10 . 20 .
;
PROC REG DATA=PREDICT;
   TITLE 'Printing Predicted Values, Residuals and Confidence Limits';
   MODEL Y = X / P R CLI CLM;
RUN;
QUIT;
```

### SOLUTION TO PROBLEM 4

```
***Data set for parts A and B;
DATA CARS;
   INFILE 'C:\WORKBOOK\CARS.DTA' PAD;
   INPUT @1  SIZE    $9.
         @38 MILEAGE  2.
         @50 RELIABLE 1.;
```

```
   IF SIZE = 'SMALL' THEN DO;
      SIZECODE = 1;
      DUMMY1 = 0;
      DUMMY2 = 0;
   END;
   ELSE IF SIZE = 'COMPACT' THEN DO;
      SIZECODE = 2;
      DUMMY1 = 1;
      DUMMY2 = 0;
   END;
   ELSE IF SIZE = 'MID-SIZED' THEN DO;
      SIZECODE = 3;
      DUMMY1 = 0;
      DUMMY2 = 1;
   END;
RUN;

***Part A;
PROC REG DATA=CARS;
   TITLE 'Multiple Regression Using Coded Values for Car Size';
   MODEL MILEAGE = SIZECODE RELIABLE;
RUN;
QUIT;

***Part B;
PROC REG DATA=CARS;
   TITLE 'Using Dummy Variables for Car Size';
   MODEL MILEAGE = DUMMY1 DUMMY2 RELIABLE;
RUN;
QUIT;
```

**SOLUTION TO PROBLEM 5**

```
LIBNAME WORKBOOK 'C:\WORKBOOK';
OPTIONS FMTSEARCH=(WORKBOOK);

DATA CLIN;
   SET WORKBOOK.CLINICAL;
   IF GENDER = 'M' THEN MALE = 1;
      ELSE MALE = 0;

/*-------------------------------------------------------------*
 | Clever alternative is:  MALE = (GENDER = 'M');             |
 | This assumes there are no missing or invalid values for GENDER. |
 *-------------------------------------------------------------*/
   LABEL  ID        = 'Pt. Number'
          GENDER    = 'Gender'
          DOB       = 'Date of Birth'
          VISIT     = 'Visit Date'
          HR        = 'Heart Rate'
          SBP       = 'Systolic Blood Pressure'
          DBP       = 'Diastolic Blood Pressure'
          MALE      = 'Is PT Male?';

   AGE = INT ((VISIT - DOB)/365.25);
RUN;

PROC REG DATA=CLIN;
   TITLE 'Multiple Regression Predicting SBP';
   MODEL SBP = MALE AGE HR DBP;
   MODEL SBP = MALE AGE HR DBP / SELECTION = STEPWISE;
   MODEL SBP = MALE AGE HR DBP / SELECTION = RSQUARE;
RUN;
QUIT;
```

**SOLUTION TO PROBLEM 6**

```
PROC FORMAT;
   VALUE YESNO 1='YES' 0='NO';
   VALUE AGEGROUP 1='> 70' 0='<= 70';
RUN;

DATA CPR;
   INFILE 'C:\WORKBOOK\CPR.DTA';
   INPUT SUBJECT  1-3
         V_FIB     4
         RESP      5
         AGEGROUP  6
         SURVIVE   7;

   FORMAT V_FIB RESP AGEGROUP SURVIVE YESNO.;

   LABEL V_FIB = 'Pt in V-FIB?'
         RESP  = 'Pt on Respirator?'
         AGEGROUP = 'Age >= 70?'
         SURVIVE  = 'Did Pt Survive?';

RUN;

PROC LOGISTIC DATA=CPR DESCENDING;
   TITLE 'Logistic Regression on CPR Data';
   MODEL SURVIVE = V_FIB RESP AGEGROUP /
                   SELECTION = FORWARD
                   CTABLE
                   RL;
RUN;
```

# CHAPTER 28 Random Assignment and Random Selection of Subjects

## SOLUTION TO PROBLEM 1

```
***Part A;
DATA ASSIGNA;
   DO SUBJECT = 1 TO 50;
      IF RANUNI(1357) < .5 THEN GROUP = 'A';
      ELSE GROUP = 'B';
      OUTPUT;
   END;
RUN;

PROC PRINT DATA=ASSIGNA;
   TITLE 'Random Assignment of Subjects - Method A';
   ID SUBJECT;
   VAR GROUP;
RUN;

PROC FREQ DATA=ASSIGNA;
   TITLE 'Frequencies - Method A';
   TABLES GROUP;
RUN;

***Part B;
DATA ASSIGNB;
   DO SUBJECT = 1 TO 50;
      GROUP= RANUNI(1357);
      OUTPUT;
   END;
RUN;

PROC RANK DATA=ASSIGNB OUT=BALANCE GROUPS=2;
   VAR GROUP;
RUN;

PROC FORMAT;
   VALUE GRP 0='A'  1='B';
RUN;

PROC PRINT DATA=BALANCE;
   TITLE 'Random Assignment of Subjects - Method B';
   ID SUBJECT;
   VAR GROUP;
   FORMAT GROUP GRP.;
RUN;

PROC FREQ DATA=BALANCE;
   TITLE 'Frequencies - Method B';
   TABLES GROUP;
   FORMAT GROUP GRP.;
RUN;
```

## SOLUTION TO PROBLEM 2

```
***Part A;
DATA ASSIGNA;
   DO SUBJECT = 1 TO 30;
   RANDOM = RANUNI(1357);
      IF RANDOM < .33333 THEN GROUP = 'A';
      ELSE IF .33333 LE RANDOM LE .66667 THEN GROUP = 'B';
```

```
      ELSE GROUP = 'C';
      OUTPUT;
   END;
   DROP RANDOM;
RUN;

PROC PRINT DATA=ASSIGNA;
   TITLE 'Random Assignment of Subjects - Method A';
   ID SUBJECT;
   VAR GROUP;
RUN;

PROC FREQ DATA=ASSIGNA;
   TITLE 'Frequencies - Method A';
   TABLES GROUP;
RUN;

***Part B;
DATA ASSIGNB;
   DO SUBJECT = 1 TO 30;
      GROUP= RANUNI(1357);
      OUTPUT;
   END;
RUN;

PROC RANK DATA=ASSIGNB OUT=PROB2 GROUPS=3;
   VAR GROUP;
RUN;

PROC FORMAT;
   VALUE GRP 0='A'  1='B'  2 = 'C';
RUN;

PROC PRINT DATA=PROB2;
   TITLE 'Random Assignment of Subjects - Method B';
   ID SUBJECT;
   VAR GROUP;
   FORMAT GROUP GRP.;
RUN;

PROC FREQ DATA=PROB2;
   TITLE 'Frequencies - Method B';
   TABLES GROUP;
   FORMAT GROUP GRP.;
RUN;
```

## SOLUTION TO PROBLEM 3

```
DATA BALANCE;
   DO BLOCK = 1 TO 5;
      DO I = 1 TO 10;
         SUBJECT + 1;
         GROUP = RANUNI(1357);
         OUTPUT;
      END;
   END;
RUN;

PROC SORT DATA=BALANCE;
   BY BLOCK;
RUN;
```

```
PROC RANK DATA=BALANCE OUT=PROB3 GROUPS=2;
   BY BLOCK;
   VAR GROUP;
RUN;

PROC FORMAT;
   VALUE GRP 0='A'  1='B';
RUN;

*--------------------------------------------------------------*
| Put data set back in subject order                           |
*--------------------------------------------------------------*;
PROC SORT DATA=PROB3;
   BY SUBJECT;
RUN;

PROC PRINT DATA=PROB3;
   TITLE 'Random Assignment of Subjects - Balanced Every 10';
   ID SUBJECT;
   VAR GROUP;
   FORMAT GROUP GRP.;
RUN;
```

**SOLUTION TO PROBLEM 4**

```
DATA BIG;
   DO SUBJECT = 1 TO 100;
      X = INT (RANUNI(1357)*100 + 1);
      OUTPUT;
    END;
RUN;

***Part A;
DATA SMALL;
   SET BIG;
   IF RANUNI(1357) LE .05;
RUN;

PROC PRINT DATA=SMALL;
   TITLE 'Approximate 5% Sample';
RUN;

***Part B;
*--------------------------------------------------------------*
| First assign a random number to each subject                 |
*--------------------------------------------------------------*;
DATA EXACT;
   SET BIG;
   RANDOM = RANUNI(1357);
RUN;

*--------------------------------------------------------------*
| Then sort by the random number                               |
*--------------------------------------------------------------*;
PROC SORT DATA=EXACT;
   BY RANDOM;
RUN;

*--------------------------------------------------------------*
| Take the first five observations                             |
*--------------------------------------------------------------*;
DATA SMALL;
   SET EXACT(OBS=5);
RUN;
```

```
*-------------------------------------------------------------*
| Put it back in subject order                                |
*-------------------------------------------------------------*;
PROC SORT DATA=SMALL(DROP=RANDOM);
    BY SUBJECT;
RUN;

PROC PRINT DATA=SMALL;
   TITLE 'Exact 5% Random Sample';
   RUN;
```

# CHAPTER 29

# More Advanced Statistics Projects

## SOLUTION TO PROBLEM 1

```
LIBNAME WORKBOOK 'C:\WORKBOOK';
OPTIONS FMTSEARCH=(WORKBOOK);

***Part A;
DATA CLINICAL;  ***Temporary data set;
   SET WORKBOOK.CLINICAL;
   AGE = INT ((VISIT - DOB)/365.25);
   LABEL AGE = 'Age at Time of Visit';
RUN;

***Part B;
PROC PRINT DATA=CLINICAL LABEL;
   TITLE 'Listing of the Clinical Data';
   ID ID;
   VAR GENDER DOB VISIT AGE PRIM_DX -- PREGNANT;
RUN;

***Part C;
PROC UNIVARIATE NORMAL PLOT DATA=CLINICAL;
   TITLE 'Descriptive Statistics and Tests of Normality';
   VAR HR SBP DBP AGE;
RUN;

***Part D;
PROC FREQ DATA=CLINICAL;
   TITLE "One-Way Frequencies, Two-Way Tables and Fisher's Exact Test";
   TABLES GENDER PRIM_DX SEC_DX VITAMINS;
   TABLES GENDER*VITAMINS / EXACT;
RUN;

***Part E;
PROC FREQ DATA=CLINICAL;
   TITLE 'Pregnancy Frequency for Females Only';
   WHERE GENDER = 'F';
   TABLES PREGNANT;
RUN;

***Part F;
PROC FREQ DATA=CLINICAL;
   TITLE 'Relationship Between Vitamins and Pregnancy for Females';
   WHERE GENDER = 'F';
   TABLES VITAMINS*PREGNANT / CHISQ;
RUN;

***Part G;
PROC TTEST DATA=CLINICAL;
   TITLE 'T-tests on Variables';
   CLASS GENDER;
   VAR HR SBP DBP AGE;
RUN;

***Part H;
PROC NPAR1WAY DATA=CLINICAL WILCOXON;
   TITLE 'Wilcoxon Rank Sum Test';
   CLASS GENDER;
   VAR HR SBP DBP AGE;
RUN;
```

```
***Part I;
PROC CORR DATA=CLINICAL PEARSON SPEARMAN NOSIMPLE;
   TITLE 'Correlation Matrix (Pearson and Spearman)';
   VAR HR SBP DBP AGE;
RUN;

***Part J;
PROC GLM DATA=CLINICAL;
   TITLE 'Test the Assumption of Homogeneity of Slope';
   CLASS GENDER;
   MODEL SBP DBP = AGE GENDER AGE*GENDER;
RUN;

***Part K;
PROC GLM DATA=CLINICAL;
   TITLE 'Analysis of Covariance';
   CLASS GENDER;
   MODEL SBP DBP = AGE GENDER;
   LSMEANS GENDER / PDIFF;
RUN;
QUIT;

***Part L;
DATA REGRESS;
   SET CLINICAL;
   *** Need to create a dummy numeric variable for GENDER;
   SEX = INPUT (TRANSLATE(GENDER,'01','MF'),1.);
   *** SEX will be 0 for Males 1 for Females;
RUN;

PROC REG DATA=REGRESS;
   TITLE 'Multiple Regression to Predict SBP';
   MODEL SBP = SEX DBP AGE / SELECTION=FORWARD;
RUN;
QUIT;

***Part M;
DATA DX_FREQ;
   SET CLINICAL (KEEP=PRIM_DX SEC_DX);
   DX = PRIM_DX;
   IF DX NE ' ' THEN OUTPUT;
   DX = SEC_DX;
   IF DX NE ' ' THEN OUTPUT;
   DROP PRIM_DX SEC_DX;
RUN;

PROC FREQ DATA=DX_FREQ;
   TITLE 'Diagnosis Frequencies';
   TABLES DX;
RUN;
```

## SOLUTION TO PROBLEM 2

```
***Part A;
DATA PROJECT2;
   LENGTH GROUP GENDER $ 1;
   INPUT GROUP $ GENDER $ X;
DATALINES;
A       M       5
A       M       6
A       M       7
A       F      11
A       F      13
```

```
A       F     14
B       M     15
B       M     10
B       M     11
B       F      4
B       F      6
B       F      7
;
PROC ANOVA DATA=PROJECT2;
   TITLE 'Two-way ANOVA';
   CLASS GROUP GENDER;
   MODEL X = GROUP | GENDER;
   MEANS GROUP|GENDER;
RUN;
QUIT;

***Part B;
PROC MEANS DATA=PROJECT2 NWAY NOPRINT;
   CLASS GROUP GENDER;
   VAR X;
   OUTPUT OUT=MEANS MEAN=;
RUN;

***Part C;
PROC PLOT DATA=MEANS;
   TITLE 'Interaction Plot';
   PLOT X * GROUP = GENDER;
RUN;

***Part D;
PROC SORT DATA=PROJECT2;
   BY GENDER;
RUN;

PROC TTEST DATA=PROJECT2;
   TITLE 'T-tests at each level of GENDER';
   BY GENDER;
   CLASS GROUP;
   VAR X;
RUN;

***Part E;
DATA ONEWAY;
   SET PROJECT2;
   CATEGORY = GROUP || '-' || GENDER;
RUN;

PROC ANOVA DATA=ONEWAY;
   TITLE 'One-way Analysis of Variance';
   CLASS CATEGORY;
   MODEL X = CATEGORY;
   MEANS CATEGORY / SNK;
RUN;
QUIT;
```

## SOLUTION TO PROBLEM 3

```
***Part A;
DATA TWOWAY;
   LENGTH GROUP $ 1;
   INPUT GROUP $ RESP;
   SUBJECT + 1;
```

```
DATALINES;
A 16
A 20
A 18
B 24
B 22
B 28
B 18
;
PROC TTEST DATA=TWOWAY;
   CLASS GROUP;
   VAR RESP;
RUN;

***Part B;
DATA TWOWAY;
   LENGTH GROUP $ 1;
   INPUT GROUP $ RESP @@;
   SUBJECT + 1;
DATALINES;
A 16  A 20   A 18   B 24   B 22   B 28   B 18
;
PROC TTEST DATA=TWOWAY;
   CLASS GROUP;
   VAR RESP;
RUN;

***Part C;
*-------------------------------------------------------------*
| This program is straightforward but not as elegant as the   |
| alternative program that follows.                           |
*-------------------------------------------------------------*;
DATA TWOWAY;
   LENGTH GROUP $ 1;
   INPUT GROUP $ @;
      DO I = 1 TO 3;
         INPUT RESP @;
         SUBJECT + 1;
         OUTPUT;
      END;
   INPUT GROUP $ @;
      DO I = 1 TO 4;
         INPUT RESP @;
         SUBJECT + 1;
         OUTPUT;
      END;
   DROP I;
DATALINES;
A 16 20 18
B 24 22 28 18
;
PROC TTEST DATA=TWOWAY;
   CLASS GROUP;
   VAR RESP;
RUN;

 /*---------------------------------------------------------*
  | Alternative Program: Shorter and more elegant than the |
  | previous program.                                      |
  |                                                        |
  | DATA TWOWAY;                                           |
  |    LENGTH GROUP $ 1;                                   |
```

```
|    DO LIMIT = 3,4;                                        |
|       INPUT GROUP $ @;                                    |
|       DO I = 1 TO LIMIT;                                  |
|          INPUT RESP @;                                    |
|          SUBJECT + 1;                                     |
|          OUTPUT;                                          |
|       END;                                                |
|    END;                                                   |
|    DROP I LIMIT;                                          |
| DATALINES;                                                |
| A 16 20 18                                                |
| B 24 22 28 18                                             |
| ;                                                         |
| PROC TTEST DATA=TWOWAY;                                   |
|    CLASS GROUP;                                           |
|    VAR RESP;                                              |
| RUN;                                                      |
*-----------------------------------------------------------*/

***Part D;
DATA TWOWAY;
   DO GROUP = 'A','B';
      IF GROUP = 'A' THEN N = 3;
      ELSE IF GROUP = 'B' THEN N = 4;
      DO I = 1 TO N;
         INPUT RESP @;
         SUBJECT + 1;
         OUTPUT;
      END;
   END;
   DROP I N;
DATALINES;
16 20 18 24 22 28 18
;
PROC TTEST DATA=TWOWAY;
   CLASS GROUP;
   VAR RESP;
RUN;

***Part E;
DATA TWOWAY;
   DO GROUP = 'A','B';
      INPUT N @;
      DO I = 1 TO N;
         INPUT RESP @;
         SUBJECT + 1;
         OUTPUT;
      END;
   END;
   DROP I N;
DATALINES;
3 16 20 18 4 24 22 28 18
;
PROC TTEST DATA=TWOWAY;
   CLASS GROUP;
   VAR RESP;
RUN;

***Part F;
DATA TWOWAY;
```

```
*-------------------------------------------------------------*
| Retain GROUP, declare it a character variable of one byte   |
*-------------------------------------------------------------*;
   LENGTH GROUP $ 1;
   RETAIN GROUP;
   INPUT DUMMY $ @@;
   IF DUMMY IN ('A','B') THEN DO;
      GROUP = DUMMY;
      DELETE;
   END;

*-------------------------------------------------------------*
| We do not need an ELSE here because of the DELETE statement |
| in the DO group above.  Following the DELETE, the DATA step |
| will return to the top and a new data value will be read.   |
*-------------------------------------------------------------*;

   RESP = INPUT (DUMMY,3.);
   SUBJECT + 1;
   DROP DUMMY;
DATALINES;
A 16 B 24 22 A 20 18 B 28 18
;
PROC TTEST DATA=TWOWAY;
   CLASS GROUP;
   VAR RESP;
RUN;

***Part G;
DATA TWOWAY;
   LENGTH GROUP $ 1;
   INPUT GROUP $ N @;
   DO I = 1 TO N;
      INPUT RESP @;
      SUBJECT + 1;
      OUTPUT;
   END;
   DROP I N;
DATALINES;
A 3 16 20 18
B 4 24 22 28 18
;
PROC TTEST DATA=TWOWAY;
   CLASS GROUP;
   VAR RESP;
RUN;
```

### SOLUTION TO PROBLEM 4

```
LIBNAME WORKBOOK 'C:\WORKBOOK';
OPTIONS FMTSEARCH=(WORKBOOK);

***Part A;
DATA HOSPITAL;
   SET WORKBOOK.CLINICAL;
   AGE = ROUND (('01JAN96'D - DOB)/365.25);
   IF 0 LE AGE LE 40 THEN AGE_GRP = 1;
      ELSE IF 41 LE AGE LE 65 THEN AGE_GRP = 2;
      ELSE IF AGE GT 65 THEN AGE_GRP = 3;
   LOG_SBP = LOG(SBP);
RUN;
```

```
***Part B;
PROC FREQ DATA=HOSPITAL;
   TITLE 'Testing Proportions';
   TABLES GENDER*VITAMINS / CHISQ;
RUN;

***Part C;
PROC TTEST DATA=HOSPITAL;
   TITLE 'Comparing Means';
   CLASS GENDER;
   VAR SBP LOG_SBP;
RUN;

PROC NPAR1WAY DATA=HOSPITAL;
   CLASS GENDER;
   VAR SBP LOG_SBP;
RUN;

***Part D;
PROC UNIVARIATE DATA=HOSPITAL;
   TITLE 'Univariate Statistics for Females Only';
   WHERE GENDER = 'F'; /* Easier than creating a new data set */
   VAR HR;
RUN;

***Part E;
PROC ANOVA DATA=HOSPITAL;
   TITLE 'One-way ANOVA';
   CLASS AGE_GRP;
   MODEL SBP LOG_SBP = AGE_GRP;
   MEANS AGE_GRP / DUNCAN;
RUN;
```

## SOLUTION TO PROBLEM 5

```
***Part A;
PROC FORMAT;
*-------------------------------------------------------------*
| Putting a space before the Y will cause the Y value to come |
| before the N in alphabetical order.                         |
*-------------------------------------------------------------*;
   VALUE YESNO 0 = 'NO' 1 = ' YES';
RUN;

DATA UNPAIRED;
   INPUT SUBJ_ID MATCH_ID GROUP $ A B C X;
DATALINES;
1       11      CASE    1    0    1    23
2        .      CASE    1    1    1    33
3       12      CASE    1    1    0    28
4       14      CASE    1    1    1    29
5       18      CASE    0    1    1    33
6       23      CASE    1    0    0    77
7       24      CASE    0    0    0    20
11       1      CONT    0    0    0    41
12       3      CONT    1    0    0    29
13       .      CONT    0    1    1    55
14       4      CONT    0    0    0    56
18       5      CONT    0    0    0    32
24       7      CONT    1    1    1    66
;
PROC PRINT DATA=UNPAIRED;
   TITLE 'Listing of data set UNPAIRED';
RUN;
```

```
PROC FREQ DATA=UNPAIRED;
   TITLE 'Unpaired Analysis of the Data';
   TABLES (A B C)*GROUP / CHISQ;
RUN;

PROC NPAR1WAY DATA=UNPAIRED WILCOXON;
   CLASS GROUP;
   VAR X;
RUN;

***Part B;
DATA CASES(RENAME=(A=CASE_A B=CASE_B C=CASE_C X=CASE_X))
     CONTROLS(RENAME=(A=CONT_A B=CONT_B C=CONT_C
                      X=CONT_X MATCH_ID=SUBJ_ID SUBJ_ID=OLD_SUBJ));
   SET UNPAIRED(WHERE=(MATCH_ID NE .));
   IF GROUP = 'CASE' THEN OUTPUT CASES;
   ELSE IF GROUP = 'CONT' THEN OUTPUT CONTROLS;
RUN;

PROC SORT DATA=CASES;
   BY SUBJ_ID;
RUN;

PROC SORT DATA=CONTROLS;
   BY SUBJ_ID;
RUN;

DATA PAIRED;
   MERGE CASES(IN=IN_CASE)
         CONTROLS(IN=IN_CONT);
   BY SUBJ_ID;
   IF IN_CASE AND IN_CONT;
   DIFF_X = CASE_X - CONT_X;
RUN;

PROC PRINT DATA=PAIRED;
   TITLE 'Listing of PAIRED';
RUN;

***Part C;
PROC FREQ DATA=PAIRED ORDER=FORMATTED;
   TITLE "McNemar's Test";
   TABLES CASE_A * CONT_A
          CASE_B * CONT_B
          CASE_C * CONT_C / AGREE;
RUN;

PROC UNIVARIATE DATA=PAIRED;
   TITLE 'Wilcoxon Signed Rank Test';
   VAR DIFF_X;
RUN;
```

# CHAPTER 30 SAS® Puzzles

## SOLUTION TO PROBLEM 1

Notice that there is no OUTPUT or RETAIN statement in this program.

A. I = 7. The DO loop counter is incremented first and then checked against the upper limit. In this program, since there is no OUTPUT statement, the first observation gets written to data set PUZZLE1 only after the DO loop has finished.

B. 1 observation. Again, because of the missing OUTPUT statement.

C. SUBJECT is missing. Because there is no RETAIN statement, SUBJECT is initially missing and remains missing (missing + 1 is always missing).

## SOLUTION TO PROBLEM 2

COUNTER is equal to 1 for each of the three observations. Several problems in this chapter are tricky since many people think of _N_ as an observation counter. In this problem, you run out of data before the DO loop even finishes once. Therefore, _N_ is equal to 1 for each of the three observations.

## SOLUTION TO PROBLEM 3

```
OBS     X     Y

 1      1     .
 2      8     .
 3      2     .
 4     10     8
 5     15    10
```

This problem is a vivid example of what can happen when you conditionally execute the LAG function. Remember that the LAG function returns the value of the argument the last time the LAG function was executed. In this example, X is greater than or equal to 5 for observations 2, 4, and 5. Thus, the first time Y has a value is in observation 4 where it "remembers" the value of 8 (the value of X in observation 2).

## SOLUTION TO PROBLEM 4

There are three observations as shown here

```
OBS    I

 1     2
 2     4
 3     6
```

When I = 1, I + 1 is 2. When the DO loop executes the second time, I is incremented and is equal to 3. I + 1 then becomes 4. For the third observation the DO loop increments I again to 5 and I + 1 results in a value of 6. I is incremented again and since the value is greater than 5, the program ends.

## SOLUTION TO PROBLEM 5

```
OBS    X

 1     1
 2     3
 3     1
```

Since this program uses IF stataments instead of ELSE-IF statements, an X value of 1 causes X to be temporarily s to 5. However, the last IF statement is then true and X gets set back to 1. There is no test for X = 3 so that value is n changed. The last X value of 5 gets set back to 1 by the last IF statement.

## SOLUTION TO PROBLEM 6

Here are the 9 observations

| OBS | A | B | FIRST_A | FIRST_B | LAST_A | LAST_B |
|---|---|---|---|---|---|---|
| 1 | 1 | 1 | 1 | 1 | 0 | 1 |
| 2 | 1 | 2 | 0 | 1 | 0 | 1 |
| 3 | 1 | 3 | 0 | 1 | 1 | 1 |
| 4 | 2 | 1 | 1 | 1 | 0 | 1 |
| 5 | 2 | 2 | 0 | 1 | 0 | 1 |
| 6 | 2 | 3 | 0 | 1 | 1 | 1 |
| 7 | 3 | 1 | 1 | 1 | 0 | 1 |
| 8 | 3 | 2 | 0 | 1 | 0 | 1 |
| 9 | 3 | 3 | 0 | 1 | 1 | 1 |

## SOLUTION TO PROBLEM 7

The RETAIN statement will have no effect since you are reading in a new value of X for each observation. The va ues of X are 1, missing, 2, missing, and 3.

## SOLUTION TO PROBLEM 8

Since there is only a single trailing at sign (@), there will be only one observatio (X=1, Y=2).

## SOLUTION TO PROBLEM 9

```
DATA PUZZLE9;
   SET CLIFTON;
   NEWVAR = AGE + 20*(GENDER='M') + 30*(GENDER='F');
RUN;
```

## SOLUTION TO PROBLEM 10

```
DATA PUZZLE10;
   INPUT LINE $80.;
   COUNT = LENGTH(COMPRESS(LINE,' .,!?'));
DATALINES;
This is a test, this is only a TEST!!!
aaa bbb     ...,,,xxx
;
```

## SOLUTION TO PROBLEM 11

```
Lengths are: A = 1   (defined by the LENGTH statement)
             B = 8   (the default in list directed input)
             C = 10  (defined by the LENGTH statement)
             D = 200 (no LENGTH statement so maximum length set)
             E = 10  (same as C)
             F = 19  (1 + 8 + 10)
```

## SOLUTION TO PROBLEM 12

N has a value of 4 in the last observation (there are 12 observations). Remember that _N_ counts iterations of th DATA step. There are 12 data values with 3 being read with each iteration of the DATA step. Therefore, the DATA step iterates 4 times.

### SOLUTION TO PROBLEM 13

```
TAX  = .15 * INCOME * (GROUP = 'A') +
       .27 * INCOME * (GROUP = 'B') +
       .35 * INCOME * (GROUP = 'C');
```

### SOLUTION TO PROBLEM 14

The value of LOGIC is `True`. The reason for this is that the logical statement is calculating the value of two quantities: X = 1 and 2. Since 2 is always true (any numeric value not 0 or missing is true), the expression must always be true, regardless of the value of X.

### SOLUTION TO PROBLEM 15

```
X_SMOKE = (SMOKE = 'Y');
```